Poverty before Politics
COLIN CLARK

1. Social security benefits now discourage people from working. It is surprising that 'voluntary' unemployment is not more prevalent.
2. The *impasse* requires drastic surgery. A reverse income tax should replace unemployment, sickness, retirement and other social security benefits, reduce personal income taxes in all income groups, particularly families with children, with a maximum marginal rate of 50 per cent, and abolish employees' national insurance contributions.
3. Below 'basic' incomes no tax would be payable. Families with less would receive reverse taxes of 7/10ths of the gap.
4. Incomes and entitlement to reverse taxes would be calculated annually; families with temporary unemployment or sickness would receive immediate assistance, adjusted at the end of the year.
5. Older people could also buy indexed government bonds to yield additional income, at less than cost if they own little property.
6. The scheme would be introduced gradually. Existing taxpayers at their request and new taxpayers automatically would be transferred to a new category paying tax at much lower rates and not paying national insurance contributions but re-nouncing social security benefits and with new claims to reverse taxes.
7. Taxpayers claiming reverse taxes for long periods would be required to show medical certificates or undergo work tests.
8. Reverse taxes would be paid only to people with low incomes. They thus differ from other methods of ensuring minimum incomes that are paid to people with middling and even higher incomes.
9. The object is for reverse taxes not only to dispense with social benefits in cash but also ultimately to enable people to pay for social benefits in kind.
10. As they showed in the 19th century, the British people can be trusted to learn how to handle their money to provide welfare for themselves. The welfare state interrupted this process by discouraging self-provision and by the inflation that has attacked the savings and insurance of people too poor to hold assets in other forms.

Hobart Paper 73 is published (price £1.50) by

THE INSTITUTE OF ECONOMIC AFFAIRS

2 Lord North Street, Westminster

London SW1P 3LB   Telephone: 01-799 3745

IEA PUBLICATIONS

Subscription Service

An annual subscription to the IEA ensures that all regular publications are sent without further charge immediately on publication—representing a substantial saving.

The cost (including postage) to subscribers in Britain is £10·00 for twelve months (£9·50 by Banker's Order). A reduction to £7·50 is made for teachers and students who pay *personally*. The overseas subscription is US $30, or the equivalent in other currencies.

To : The Treasurer,
     Institute of Economic Affairs,
     2 Lord North Street,
     Westminster,
     London SW1P 3LB

Please register an individual subscription of £10·00 (£7·50 for teachers and students who pay *personally*) for the twelve months beginning. . . . .

☐   Remittance enclosed   ☐ Please send invoice

☐   I should prefer to pay by Banker's Order which reduces the subscription to £9·50.

Name . . . .

Address. . . . .

       . . . .

Position. . . . .

Signed . . . .

Date . . . .

HP73

PREFACE

The *Hobart Papers* are intended to contribute a stream of authoritative, independent and lucid analysis to the understanding and application of economics to private and government activity. Their characteristic theme has been the optimum use of scarce resources and the extent to which it can best be achieved in markets within an appropriate framework of laws and institutions or, where markets are inoperable, by other methods.

The nature and kinds of 'market failure' have been anxiously analysed by economists for 200 years since Adam Smith. The nature and kinds of 'government failure' have been discussed only in the last 15 or 20 years. That may be why economists and others concerned about the imperfections of markets in maximising output and distributing it equitably have been inclined to argue it is necessary only to demonstrate that markets are imperfect to make the case for replacing them by government in producing and distributing goods and services. Professor Harold Demsetz of the University of Chicago described this optical illusion as 'the *nirvana* approach'.[1]

Perhaps the most damaging criticism of the market, made especially by sociologists rather than economists as broad groups, though each with individual exceptions, has been that it fails to distribute income equally, or at least equitably enough to enable everyone to pay for the goods and services thought desirable for civilised living. Poverty and inequality have been the accusations most commonly made against the market. They are the criticisms that have substantially influenced thinking on social policy and produced variants of the Welfare State that has been developed to its highest degree in Britain, apart from the forms it takes in Communist countries. Its principle is that, in order to avoid poverty and ensure equality, goods and services shall be provided not through the market and paid for in prices but by government and provided 'free' or at prices subsidised from taxation.

Other IEA *Papers*, beginning from the early days of the Institute, have demonstrated the economic *non sequitur* in this development of economic thinking and policy: that to remedy the deficiency or inequity on the side of *demand* it did not follow

[1] 'Information and Efficiency', *Journal of Law and Economics*, April 1969.

that the remedy had to be on the side of *supply*. In Hobart Paper 73 Dr Colin Clark examines the alternative correction to inadequacy or inequality in income: to deal with it directly by topping-up low incomes (or supplying income to people with none), thus leaving the supply of goods and services to be provided through market, which even its economist critics usually concede had advantages of choice for consumers between competing suppliers that were not available in systems of supply by government.

Even before the Institute began in 1957 Dr Clark, one of its earliest advisers and never-failing stalwarts, had questioned the conventional welfare state approach, specifically in a short book, *Welfare and Taxation*, in 1954. He showed that the Welfare State was raising vast sums in taxation (including social insurance) and returning it to taxpayers who could have been left with it to pay for welfare services of their choice. As in the statistics of national income and outlay, his private, fertile pioneering led, after the customary bureaucratic delay, to official statistics now published annually in *Economic Trends* that largely confirm the conclusion he then reached. Economists will recall the statement of Alfred Marshall that if the State does something well it is usually based on an idea started by a private individual.

The solution to this vast structure of financial coals-to-Newcastle, which post-war governments of both parties have allowed to develop under the pressure of electoral support-seeking, is an idea originated privately by another fertile economist, Professor Milton Friedman: the negative (in Britain reverse) income tax. Inspired by these two pioneers, the Institute from its early days sponsored studies of methods by which people with low incomes would be enabled to pay for welfare services alongside those who earned sufficient in the market. The most recent such study was *Policy for Poverty* in 1970,[1] in which several forms of topping-up were examined by a small IEA group for which the researches were done by the late George Polanyi to whose memory Dr Clark's *Paper* is dedicated.

Dr Clark has divided his *Paper* into six parts. The first outlines briefly the antecedents to the degeneration of methods

---

[1] The Report of an IEA Study Group: Anthony Christopher, George Polanyi, Arthur Seldon, Barbara Shenfield, published as Research Monograph 20, IEA, January 1970.

of helping the poor into politically-inspired social benefits for all and sundry. Part II explains how the Welfare State tax/benefit confusion has produced the 'poverty trap' in which people who try to earn a little more lose more than they earn by having to forego social benefits. Parts III and IV outline Dr Clark's proposal for a reverse tax and its costs in some detail. Part V compares his Reverse Tax with other recent proposals. And Part VI summarises the argument.

Dr Clark feels strongly that social policy has, since the war, gone more rapidly up the wrong turning that began in modern times with Bismarck and earlier. He is at variance with the general drift and thinking among British sociologists, although they will find it difficult to dismiss his argument and proposals as displaying insufficient concern for the poor, since in his early days his attempts to enter Parliament as a Labour MP were largely inspired by his wish to assist in measures that would help them. For 45 years he has illuminated economic thinking by his uncompromising analyses usually based on scrupulous documentation by statistics. Like other British economists who have left to work abroad, he can be said to have done Britain more honour than she has done him.

The argument for a reverse income tax has gained ground in the last 10 years despite the stubborn, largely emotional resistance to it from people who cannot accept that the method of the Welfare State has failed, as well as from academics and others who cannot accept that the market system is less imperfect than the method of government. It was indeed the Labour Government of 1964–70 in which Lord Houghton took the first steps towards a form of reverse income tax in its examination of a minimum income. The Conservative Government of 1970–74 went further and Sir Keith Joseph introduced an embryo reverse tax in the form of the Family Income Supplement and examined the idea further in its proposals for 'tax credits'. Then, mysteriously, the idea seems to have become lost. It might have been expected that the 1974 Labour Government would take its minimum income idea further and perhaps benefit from the experience of the Family Income Supplement and the thinking put into tax credits. But since 1974 there has been silence. Is it that the idea was considered faulty? If so, no reasons have been given. Or is the reason more questionable and cynically political? Will historians discover why the reverse income tax sank into the sands under Labour in 1974?

[5]

Dr Clark's present *Hobart Paper* follows two others, *Growth-manship* in 1961, in which he contested the conventional wisdom about the argument for industrial investment as the key to economic growth, and *Taxmanship* in 1964, in which he questioned whether rising wages or rising prices were mainly responsible for inflation and concluded by blaming excessive government spending financed out of taxes. In his present, third, *Hobart Paper* he breaks new ground by estimating the cost of a Reverse Tax as well as showing it to be the most hopeful solution for the *impasse* into which the Welfare State has developed.

Its constitution requires the Institute to dissociate its Trustees, Directors and Advisers from the analyses and recommendations of its authors, but it presents Dr Clark's *Poverty before Politics* as a stimulating statistical illustration of an idea in social policy that should gain increasing attention and acceptance, not only from economists, but also from sociologists who are prepared to acknowledge 'government failure' in the Welfare State, from politicians of all parties more concerned with the poor than with political advantage, and from observers of the continuing deterioration in British social policy.

March 1977   Arthur Seldon

CONTENTS

Front cover chart: based on figures in Table IV

THE AUTHOR

Colin Clark was born in 1905 and educated at Winchester and Brasenose College, Oxford. He holds the degrees of MA and DLitt from Oxford and MA from Cambridge.

He was Lecturer in Statistics, University of Cambridge, 1931–37; Labour parliamentary candidate in 1929, 1931 and 1935; Visiting Lecturer at the Universities of Melbourne, Sydney and Western Australia, 1937–39. He has been economic consultant to the Governments of Ceylon, India and Pakistan, and Financial Adviser to the Treasury of Queensland, Australia. Hon. Sc.D. (Milan), Hon. D.Econ (Tilburg). Director of the Institute for Research in Agricultural Economics, University of Oxford, 1953–69. Research Fellow at Monash University, Melbourne, Australia, from 1969 to 1976, when he returned to England. He is a member of the Advisory Council of the IEA.

Dr Clark's publications include *The National Income, 1924–31* (1932); *National Income and Outlay* (1937); *The Conditions of Economic Progress* (1940); *The Economics of 1960* (1942); *Welfare and Taxation* (1954); (with M. R. Haswell) *The Economics of Subsistence Agriculture* (1964); *Population Growth and Land Use* (1967); *The Economics of Irrigation* (1967); *Starvation or Plenty?* (1970); *The Value of Agricultural Land* (1973); and numerous articles in economic periodicals. For the IEA he has written *Growthmanship* (Hobart Paper 10, 1961; 2nd edition 1962); *Taxmanship* (Hobart Paper 26, 1964; 2nd edition 1970); and a paper in *The State of Taxation* (IEA Readings No. 16, 1977).

I. COMPASSION AND POLITICKING SINCE ANCIENT ROME

Diligent search by historians has failed to reveal where and how the phrase 'Welfare State' originated.

Two concepts of 'social services': double-talk

There are two conflicting concepts of social services. One is to make provision for people in real need who cannot help themselves. The other is the concept of 'something for everyone', or the Welfare State, in which not only people in need, but *everyone* looks to the state to make his normal welfare provisions for him. In the trenchant words of the *Economist*, social security was originally designed to provide a 'safety net' for families facing the danger of falling to the ground but, such is our capacity for confused thought, before long people were heard demanding 'fair shares in safety nets'.

The phrase 'the Welfare State' has become a double-talk. 'Is it not the duty of the state to see to the welfare of the people?', the questioner will indignantly ask. Of course it is. But it certainly does not follow that it is the duty of the state to provide welfare services for people who are perfectly capable of providing them for themselves. 'Nobody starves in the Welfare State' is a common catch-phrase. Those who talk in this manner display an invincible stupidity. Do they really think that there is no other way of preventing starvation?

This concept of the Welfare State has, however, an inescapable attraction for politicians. It is almost asking them to act contrary to nature for them to neglect the interests of 90 per cent of the voters in favour of the minority who are really in need.

'Nobody shoots Father Christmas' is a favourite political motto. But people would have a different attitude to a Father Christmas who came round on Boxing Day to collect the entire cost of the gifts he had handed out, together with a substantial commission for himself for having organised the distribution. The ordinary man now sees much more clearly than his leaders apparently do that the cost of all social services has to be met out of taxation, which falls heavily even on the poorest families. He is also all too well aware that part of his hard-earned wages is going in taxation to provide for people who are receiving social security benefits to which they are not entitled. Whether such 'scroungers' are many or few, he sees them as an affront to justice, and is demanding a change in the system that permits it.

It has happened before. Ancient Rome, before the time of Julius Caesar and Augustus, was a republic, with democratic voting of a sort (under a system very far from perfect). The authorities were in command of revenue, in the form of grain paid as tribute by conquered provinces. There eventuated a distribution of public welfare grain payments, not simply to people in need, but to everyone on the electoral register.

Gregorian means test

Once started, welfare state provisions are extremely hard to stop. The citizens of Rome were still expecting free distributions in the late sixth century AD, by which time the city had long lost its imperial possessions (and Britain had relapsed into barbarism). Secular and ecclesiastical authority in Rome at this time were combined in the hands of Pope Gregory the Great—a remarkable man who sent the first missionaries to pagan England, and was also a musician of genius, who gave us the Gregorian chant. In this time of confusion, he was able to lay his hands on a limited corn supply—but he found it necessary to impose a means test, the necessity for which he explained most eloquently:

> '*Neither little to whom much should be given, nor much to whom little, nor nothing to the man who should have something, or something to the man who should have nothing.*'

This maxim was translated, and acted upon, by our King Alfred the Great.

Going back to King Alfred—we could hardly go further: observe the principle that, apart from private obligations, there was also an obligation falling on public authority—in those days kings, noblemen and abbots—to provide for the poor. After what appears to have been a worsening of poverty and unemployment in the 16th century, these obligations were systematised and imposed upon public authorities, organised by parishes.

Money for all kinds of social services now comes from a distant central government, with everyone under the happy delusion that someone else is paying for them. It is a very different matter when all funds for the relief of the poor have to be raised by local rates. Then it is all too obvious who is paying for them, including the local councillors or guardians, and their immediate associates. In these circumstances every claimant is carefully investigated, and there is no doubt about the necessity of a means test. 19th-century Poor Law administration was probably sometimes unduly severe.

One small example will illustrate the stealthy and sinister process whereby provision at first designed for people in real need became transformed into a system of universal and costly hand-outs. This is the system we now call the Welfare State, with much going to families who could easily provide for themselves. Towards the end of the 19th century, after universal education had been established, sympathetic teachers found some children unable to study because they were hungry. Inquiry showed that usually their parents were in great poverty. So school meals were instituted, at first to provide for this urgent need. Then the cry arose that it was embarrassing for some children to be so segregated. Those who welcomed collective feeding for its own sake claimed that it would be administratively simpler to feed all the children together. Then there were the nutrition cranks who said that the average parents did not know how to feed their children properly. So we have ended up with a partially means-tested, costly, social service, much of which is for the benefit of comparatively wealthy families, to save them from the trouble of providing their children with sandwiches, etc., as in other countries.

Bismarck, not Lloyd George or Beveridge

The principle of social welfare payments without a means test was extensively developed in the introduction of unemployment and sickness benefits. These benefits did not originate with Lloyd George and the Liberal Government of the Edwardian era, as is widely supposed. They were first introduced, on a comprehensive scale, in Germany under Bismarck in the 1880s. Bismarck openly if cynically announced his reason: not compassion but to make the Social Democratic Party, which was then making considerable electoral advances, 'sound their bird-call to the electors in vain'. He was however, in the event, not very successful in attaining his objective. The German Social Democratic Party in those days was theoretically Marxian, though in practice its demands were extremely limited. But it is highly ironic to see the leading English Liberals

[13]

and Fabians of the Edwardian age advocating Imperial Germany as the example to follow.

There were features of these earlier schemes in Germany, and in the British schemes copied from them, which differentiated them from the present-day Welfare State. In Germany (not in Britain) they were, until the 1920s, administered locally. In both countries they were originally designed not as hand-outs but as state-subsidised insurance schemes, with actuarially controlled funds sufficient to meet all expected demands on them. Also then (as now) payments were available for only a limited period. Those who fell out of benefit had to rely, at that time, on the Poor Law. Local administration of the Poor Law began to break down under the heavy long-term unemployment of the 1920s, which hit some municipalities very much harder than others, and now has been replaced by the Supplementary Benefits Commission (SBC). But in each case the applicant for support has had to face a means test.

There was another important difference from the present-day system of universal benefits. National Insurance in Britain was confined to people earning below £5 per week, which, in those days, meant most manual workers but only the lower-paid salaried workers. People earning above this income, including those working on their own account, were expected to be able to make their own provision for unemployment and sickness.

Emotional opposition to measuring means

It is hard to explain the juxtaposition of the intense emotional opposition still aroused by the idea of a means test with its now widespread acceptance in practice. Means-testing is, of course, necessary when paying out public funds for the relief of poverty. The amount available for such purposes is inevitably limited, and if much of it is handed out without a means test to those who do not really need it, there will of necessity be so much less left to help people in real need. A lot of public money is still now being paid out in unemployment and sickness benefits, without means tests, to those who are not in real need of help. At the same time, as will be shown below, there is now a multiplicity of social services—over 40—in which separate means tests have to be applied, at considerable expense, and often with inconsistent results.

Simple rationality demands that there should be a single

means test. And much the best way in which it could be administered is by precisely the same method as the means of all the rest of us are tested, for income tax assessment—a careful checking of income. Just as all with incomes above a certain limit (which should of course be far higher than the present lower limit for income taxation) should be liable to pay tax, so all with incomes below it should qualify for help.

This help, moreover, should be given in the form of money. At present a bewildering variety of services, from subsidised housing downwards, are provided to families believed to be in need. Quite apart from the consideration that many of these services go to families not really entitled to them, and confining our attention to families who really are in need, providing them with a miscellany of goods and services specified by Parliament at various times is vastly inferior to providing them with the cash. A good deal of administrative expense could thus be avoided. The best judge of a poor family's circumstances and requirements is itself. The best way to relieve its needs is to give it the money, and to allow it to satisfy the most urgent of them. Beneath our present welfare legislation there lies a massive contempt for the poor, who are believed to be too ignorant and feckless to know what is good for them, and require Big Brother in Parliament to decide for them.

Learning to handle money by reverse taxes

Those engaged in social work—and most members of Parliament are active social workers as well as serving their party in the lobbies—are indeed aware that there are families which are totally disorganised, feckless, cannot cope, incapable of handling money—however you like to describe it. It says much for the character of the people, and indeed we should be grateful, that there are not many more of them. For Parliament itself is largely responsible. Under governments of both parties, it has for decades now enacted one piece of legislation after another designed to free the individual family from need for responsibility or forethought in money matters. Politicians have done their utmost to create the impression that families can now afford to neglect these ancient virtues, and take life easily, because an ever-increasing number of their requirements will be looked after by the 'Welfare State'.

[15]

In the 19th century, despite what were, by our standards, low wages and considerable intermittency of employment, families were expected to have sufficient savings to meet illness, unemployment, and the normal contingencies of life, not to mention widowhood and old age.[1] Poor relief was available, but only in the direst circumstances, and families would face near-starvation before subjecting themselves to the disgrace of applying for it—or leaving their aged relatives to do so. For families above the general level, office workers and small business proprietors, it was taken for granted, practically without exception, that they would provide for contingencies themselves.

19th-century standards, it is now universally agreed, were too severe. Without our having to re-instate them in full, it nevertheless behoves us to observe what was good in them—as Alfred Marshall did, besides writing on theoretical economics. Particularly the ordinary family, even with rudimentary education, knew how to handle money, and did not spend it all as quickly as it was earned. This forethought was helped by institutions, including the Post Office Savings Bank, and many established by non-governmental initiatives, co-operative societies, trade unions which paid unemployment benefit, friendly societies, with strange names such as Oddfellows and Buffalos, that made provision for sickness.

Such private organisations are not required in the 'Welfare State', our politicians proclaim; and, instead of encouraging thrift and forethought, do everything they can to discourage them by their policy of deliberate inflation, the lowest form of political meanness and cowardice, which attacks with the greatest severity the savings deposits and insurance policies of people too poor to hold assets in other forms.

The essential concept of the policy proposed in this *Hobart Paper* is that, in place of the present patronising contempt with which Parliament tells them what is good for them, people on the contrary can be trusted to learn for themselves how to handle their money and to provide rationally for their needs by paying for welfare services as they decide. This process of

[1] [We now also know, from the evidence investigated by Professor E. G. West, that many paid school fees on a scale much larger than was commonly supposed from the writings of Charles Dickens and the other social novelists. (*Education and the State*, IEA, 1965, 2nd edition 1970; *Education and the Industrial Revolution*, Batsford, 1975.) —ED.]

learning would be facilitated and accelerated by a system of reverse taxes.

II. THE PRESENT TAX-BENEFIT DISCONTENTS

The burden of taxation and of government spending has now become overwhelming. Many suggestions for their reduction are now being made, of more or lesser value, most of them desirable. But people who write and speak on government spending and taxation show a persistent tendency to evade the most important issue. There must be a large reduction in expenditure on social security. It amounted to £9.6 billion in 1975, a 30 per cent increase on 1974, with every prospect of similar increases in the future.

To help the poor and cut taxes

The proposals in this *Hobart Paper*, while making better provision than now for the genuinely poor, are designed to provide for large reductions in taxation. Unemployment and sickness benefits in their present form, of which much goes to people not in real need, must be progressively abolished, and supplementary benefits replaced by a system which will help the working poor as well as the unemployed and pensioners.

The tax reductions expected to be made possible by these reforms may in part take the form of the abolition of employees' National Insurance contributions and of several alternative revised scales of income tax shown below: but in addition there will remain substantial funds available for reducing taxation elsewhere.

A further aim, eventually but no less important, is to enable people to pay for what are now childishly called 'free' welfare and possibly other goods and services.

The trouble is not only that the expense of social security has become inordinate. Under our present system we are paying people not to work. We are now faced with the unprecedented conjuncture of high unemployment with difficulties in increasing output, labour shortages in key sectors, and rapid inflation.

Unemployment and the 'poverty trap'

Economists steeped in obsolete forms of thought going back to the 1930s cannot explain this combination of inflation and

[17]

unemployment. (They call themselves Keynesians though Keynes would have been the first to disavow their thinking had he still been living.) The truth is that a good deal of unemployment is, in varying degrees, 'voluntary'. Indeed, it says much for many men's sense of scruple that there is not a good deal more 'voluntary unemployment', particularly among men with several dependent children, when we study Chart A (page 19). The diagrams in Chart A show the position as it was in November 1976. The changes in tax exemptions in the March 1977 Budget (but not taking into account the conditional reduction in standard rate from 35 to 33 per cent which may come into force later in the year), and the revised children's allowances, but with all other conditions unchanged, will offset employed men's net family incomes as follows:

	Change in tax allowances	Effects on net income	Loss of old Family Allowance (net of tax)	New Child Benefit (untaxed)	Total net increase
	£/year	£/week	£/week	£/week	£/week
Single person	70	0.47			0.47
Married couple	140	0.94			0.94
Married couple					
+ 1 child	36	0.24		1.00	1.24
+ 2 children	−94	−0.63	−0.97	2.50	0.90
+ 4 children	−354	−2.38	−2.93	5.50	0.19

The unemployed man's family, on the other hand, will gain the fourth column and lose the third column *gross* of tax, amounting to slightly more net gain than the employed man's, i.e. extending the poverty trap!

The comparative advantages of not working become even more when tax refunds are taken into account. In giving the reply on which Chart A is based,[1] the Minister for Social

[1] *Hansard*, 15 October 1976, cols. 245–250.

ASSUMED EXPENSES £ PER WEEK (CHART A)

	Single and childless couple	Married couple with 1 child	Married couple with 2 children	Married couple with 4 children
Work expenses	1.75	1.75	1.75	1.75
Rent	3.93	4.51	4.72	5.38
Rates	1.58	1.83	1.90	2.18

Source: *Hansard*, 15 October 1970, Cols. 245-250

CHART A.
EMPLOYED & UNEMPLOYED*:NET WEEKLY SPENDING POWER

*3–28weeks

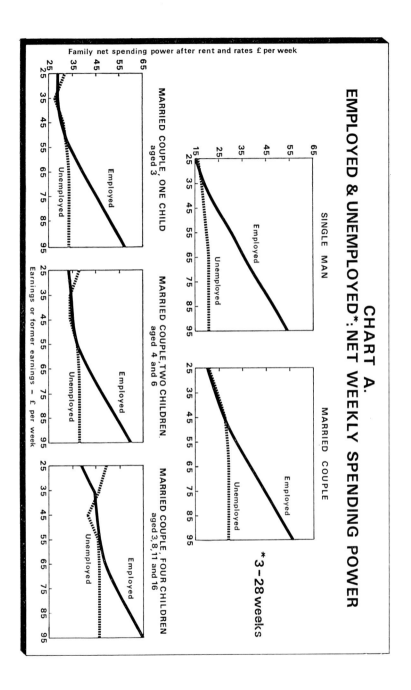

Family net spending power after rent and rates £ per week

SINGLE MAN

Employed

Unemployed

MARRIED COUPLE

Employed

Unemployed

MARRIED COUPLE, ONE CHILD aged 3

Employed

Unemployed

MARRIED COUPLE, TWO CHILDREN aged 4 and 6

Employed

Unemployed

MARRIED COUPLE, FOUR CHILDREN aged 3, 8, 11 and 16

Employed

Unemployed

Earnings or former earnings – £ per week

Security, Mr Stanley Orme, excluded tax refunds from the calculation on the following grounds:

'It is not realistic to regard tax refunds as part of the regular weekly income of an unemployed person, since he does not automatically receive these refunds, and when payments are made, they usually occur at monthly intervals. Moreover the payment of tax refunds will depend not only on the point of time in a tax year but also on the number of weeks of employment during the tax year.'

Where, however, as in many cases, tax refunds are also receivable, the Minister stated the approximate weekly amount of such refunds as follows:

	Approximate weekly amount of tax refund (1976–77 tax levels) £
Single person	4.95
Married couple	7.30
Married couple + 1 child aged 3	9.35
Married couple + 2 children aged 4 and 6	10.50
Married couple + 4 children aged 3, 8, 11 and 16	13.45

(Receipt of tax refunds may affect entitlement to free school meals but not other means-tested benefits.)

Even without tax refunds, a wage of £55 per week now offers little net increase over social security payments, except for single men. When tax refunds are payable, stories of men refusing to accept even an £80 wage become credible.

This information was provided in Parliament thanks to the persistence of Mr Ralph Howell, MP, whose trenchant pamphlet, *Why Work?: A Challenge to the Chancellor,*[1] describes the animated and well-informed discussions in the bar of the Black Horse Inn in a Norfolk village, where men upright enough to continue working regularly have been subjected to ridicule, because 'a man with wife and two children, earning £40 per week (1975 wages) is left with a spending power of £28.72 when working, and £40.39 when in the first weeks of unemployment' (taking into account the tax rebates receivable during these weeks).

[1] Conservative Political Centre, London, 1976.

What is sometimes called the 'poverty trap' is equally strongly condemned by Mr Howell's political opponents:

'The fall in the tax threshold to below the official poverty line . . . entanglement between taxes and social security benefits, created by the fact that the concept of poverty is ignored in the administration of tax policy, has a destructive effect on the living standards of the low-paid . . . the "poverty trap" . . . The family may well end up better off without a pay rise.' [1]

The issue was stated in still more dramatic form by the *Economist*: [2]

'Who pays the highest rate of tax on every extra £ he earns? Not, under Britain's crazy tax and welfare system, the millionaire, but the family man earning £1,500–£2,200 a year.'

A single earner, with between £805 (at which very low figure income tax becomes payable) and about £2,000, pays, in effect, about two-thirds of every additional pound he or she earns, through the workings of the national insurance contribution, income tax and means-tested rent and rate rebates. But it is much worse for a married man with two children. From an income of £1,591 (at which he begins to pay income tax) for a considerable range he is shown as *worse off* for each additional £ he earns, through the combined operation of income taxation, employees' contribution, and the reduction of means-tested benefits. This calculation assumes he gets all (or nearly all) the means-tested benefits, and that they are all cut off or reduced the moment his earnings rise. In practice the situation is modified—Family Income Supplement (FIS) runs for 12 months, school meals for at least a term, and so on.

Nevertheless the situation is approximately as described. It arises from the interaction of a medley of means-tested welfare schemes; and also by the crowning absurdity of imposing income tax and national insurance contributions on families clearly below the poverty line.

The *Economist*'s table does not take into account unemployment benefit and supplementary benefit which families with low incomes may usually be expected to be receiving. But, apart from these benefits, it is of interest to show the earnings

---

[1] Chris Pond, Frank Field and Steve Winyard, *Trade Unions and Taxation*, Workers' Educational Association, June 1976, pp. 2–3.

[2] 'Business Brief: Tax and poverty', 24 July 1976, p. 60. In the paragraph that follows the figures have again been amended to take account of the changes in the exemptions provided in the March 1977 Budget.

at which the various taxes and benefits come into operation for a low-income married man with two children under 11, with wife not earning (Table I).

(Unemployment benefit is treated as 'earnings' in the assessment of all benefits except FIS and family allowance.)

TABLE I

EARNINGS CUT-OFF POINTS FOR TAXES AND BENEFITS[1]

Gross earnings £ per week	Present provisions	Net spending power £ per week
0	Family Allowance, FIS, rent, rates, school meals and health charges rebates	18.2
13	National Insurance contribution payable	30.4
20	Rent rebate starts to fall	37.1
20.6	Rate rebate starts to fall	37.5
24	Family Income Supplement starts to fall	39.5
29.8	Income tax payable	41.2
32.2	Change in rent and rate rebate calculations	41.0
41.9	Cessation of FIS, reduction of rebates on school meals, prescriptions, etc.	39.5
51.1	Cessation of rate rebate	42.8
53.4	Cessation of rent rebate	43.6

'Furthermore to make possible this lunatic overlap of the tax and social security systems we are having to employ more and more civil servants . . . It is not widely realised that about half of the present civil service—outside the defence services—is now engaged in collecting taxes and making transfer payments, in many cases from and to the very same person.'[2]

The United States also has such problems. 'Welfare' payments are usually subject to a 100 per cent cut-out rate for any family earnings. And the situation may be even worse in legislation for publicly-financed medical care, which in some circumstances 'can turn a rise in hourly earnings into a financial disaster, and can make a decision to work longer hours a kind of financial suicide'.[3]

Wastes of state welfare: the SBC . . .

For a hundred years or more Parliament has been enacting measure after measure with the laudable object of using public funds to help the poor. The consequences of these measures in practice, however, have been

[1] This Table requires slight revision in view of the raising of the point at which income tax becomes payable from £29.8 to £30.5 in the March 1977 Budget.
[2] Colin Jones, 'The Need to Tackle Whitehall Growth at the Roots', *Financial Times*, 31 July 1976.
[3] H. J. Aaron, *Why is Welfare so Hard to Reform?*, The Brookings Institution, Washington DC, 1973, pp. 15–16.

—to incur inordinate costs,

—to transfer large sums of public money to people who do not
need help,

—to blunt or even reverse incentives,

—to provide employment for an army of administrators—while
still leaving many families hard pressed.

The policy of governments in recent years has been to attempt to deal with outstanding problems of poverty through the Supplementary Benefits Commission.[1] At the end of 1975 it was employing a staff of 91,300, providing supplementary benefits to 2,793,000 people, of whom 60 per cent were pensioners and 20 per cent unemployed. The annual cost of payments to supplementary benefit claimants at the rates applying at the end of 1975 was £1,420 million (p. 97), and the costs of administering them £190 million, or nearly $13\frac{1}{2}$ per cent.

The number of 'exceptional circumstances additions' rose from 425,000 in 1971 to 1,090,000 in 1975, and of 'exceptional needs payments' from 386,000 in 1967 to 576,000 in 1971 and 945,000 in 1975 (pp. 61–63).

Parliament has instructed the Commission to deal with poor families' 'exceptional needs'. This instruction is becoming more and more difficult to carry out. Difficulties began with pensioners and others who found they could not meet heating costs; by December 1975 they had made no less than 915,000 claims (p. 23). Then there was help to purchase children's clothes: 'Is that an equitable and self-respecting way of clothing children?', ask the Commission (p. 12). So it goes on—down to the cost of removing dead elm trees from backyards.

Inevitably, to an increasing degree, officials have to be given discretionary powers. Then (pp. 12–13)

'conflict follows between claimants and officials, between claimant and claimant, and between claimants and the public: the letters of complaint which people write to their MPs and to the Commission often quote comparisons with the treatment someone else has received'.

So the Commission set out to draft more and more elaborate rules in an attempt to secure *uniformity* in the treatment of every *exceptional* case.

[1] Its *Annual Report* for 1975 was published in 1976 (Cmnd. 6615). All the figures and quotations in this section are from the 1975 Report.

'More and more problems have to be referred upwards to regional
headquarters for decisions and volumes of instructions have been
compiled so long, so complex and so frequently amended that
officials themselves often find them very difficult to understand.'

And

'because the instructions are unpublished there is an unwarranted
suspicion of their contents, and this provokes unnecessary
conflicts'.

Discretion, because it makes decisions harder, and calls for
experienced officials and a lot of visiting, is very expensive in
staff to administer properly, yet still 'we cannot be sure that it
gets help to all those in the greatest need'.

. . . and injustices, abuses and hostility

The present system is also unjust.

'Many of the working poor', the Commission add, 'who get no
supplementary benefit because they are in full-time jobs, also
have difficulty in paying for their fuel, visiting their relatives in
hospital, and so on, and some of them resent it when they find
that Supplementary Benefit Commission claimants get help with
such things—help towards which they contribute.'

Indeed, the extremely low level of income on which taxation
is now imposed not only provides a disincentive to claimants
considering a return to work, but also 'provokes hostility among
the low-paid workers towards our claimants and the benefits
which support them' (p. 15).

The Commission (p. 58) made direct payments of rent for
26,000 people in 1974, and for 51,000 in 1975. It is not at all
happy about this. Claimants should be

'as free as any other member of the community to manage their
finances and accept the responsibility for their actions, even if
these lead to eviction. The danger of paying rent direct is that
the claimant and his family will cease to see rent as a personal
responsibility and will regard it as an automatic right which
requires no action from them.'

There were also no fewer than 2,261,000 householders in
December 1975 (81 per cent of all claimants) receiving additional benefit for their rent (p. 55). The rules for assessing rent
assistance are unduly complex, and there is an awkward
overlap between supplementary benefits and rent rebates on

council houses granted by local authorities. Unreasonably high claims for rent assistance, it is admitted (p. 56), are rarely questioned.

The rules (pp. 23–24) for 'disregard' of income and capital resources are also confused.

Cradle-to-grave services?—or minimum income?

Finally, the Commission come to questioning (p. 16) the very basis of their existence:

> 'Should we do our best to help our claimants cope with every aspect of their lives and secure all the services that they may need, or should we confine ourselves to providing an assured minimum of income?'

What the Commission says is right. We are now incurring inordinate expense in administering, not only Supplementary Benefits, but a whole host of other means-tested schemes (below). But the stronger condemnation of our present policy is that we are giving poor families not what they judge their most urgent needs but what politicians and bureaucrats think they most need.

The poor know their needs best

We must start from the obvious proposition that the funds available for social security are limited. Those who best understand the most urgent needs to which these limited funds should be devoted are not the politicians and the bureaucrats, but the poor themselves. The funds available should not be parcelled out, in this wasteful and incoherent manner, among rent subsidies, rate subsidies, school meal subsidies, and all the rest. They should be distributed, *in cash*, to families in poverty, who in general make the best judgement—far better than anyone else can make for them—of what goods and services they stand most in need, and will then be able to purchase these goods and services at ordinary prices.

Social surgery drastic

The surgery required will be drastic. Once adequate provision had been made for families in need, unemployment and sickness benefits, much of which now go to families not in need, would have to be abolished. Likewise the SBC would have to go. If you reintroduce it to deal with 'exceptional cases', before you know where you are everyone's case will be 'exceptional'. The preservation of unemployment and sickness benefits, and of the SBC, are political necessities, we shall be told, as if such a statement were final. 'Political necessities', said Sir Dennis Robertson the economist, 'are something which only a wealthy country can afford to have.'

Genuine 'exceptional needs' are a fit subject for private charity, which should be given every encouragement in the first place by a general lowering of taxation rates, together with full immediate tax-deductibility for gifts to registered charities, such as is given in the USA and Australia, without the cumbrous mechanism of covenants.

Reverse tax

Provision for those in need should be made by means of a 'Reverse Tax' (originally proposed as negative income tax by Professor Milton Friedman of Chicago).[1] A minimum standard of income should be set, taking into account numbers of dependants, above which it is reasonable to consider that income tax should be payable (something very different from our present scale, which imposes income tax on many families obviously below the poverty line). Then any family with income below the minimum standard should receive a payment from the state, based on the amount by which their income falls below the minimum standard.

Reverse Tax is by no means the same thing as Tax Credits, two recent variants of which are considered below (Section V). Reverse Tax is payable only to families demonstrably in need. Tax Credits are issued to all—or almost all—families, to be used for part or full fulfilment of tax obligations, and, insofar as they are not needed for this purpose, to be retained as a cash grant. They would have the undoubted merit of greatly simplifying tax administration—the standard rate of tax could be set high, with the tax credit automatically mitigating it for low incomes and for dependants. But tax credits could abolish poverty only if granted on an abundant and very expensive scale.

Measure of means essential to help poor

The means-test always evokes hostile reactions. But those of us

---

[1] [Now in the process of retiring to the Hoover Institution of Stanford University where he was appointed Senior Research Fellow in December 1976.—ED.]

[26]

who are not poor have annually to undergo a most searching means-test, in the form of an income tax assessment, with liability to severe penalties for concealing any source of income, however trivial. The system of income tax assessment, and the checking of information, now applies to almost every income, however low. There should be no insuperable administrative difficulty in making it apply to all incomes, and using such assessments as a basis for paying Reverse Tax to families below the minimum limit for income taxation. This minimum should clearly be fixed at a much higher level than at present.

Many people feel an intuitive hostility to the concept of a 'means-test'. But any measure which aims to benefit the poor must, of necessity, involve a means 'test', or rather a measure of means. This is common sense. The alternative policy is to give benefits to all, whether they need them or not. Such a policy, quite apart from offending against both justice and economics, also means that the available funds will, inevitably, be so widely stretched that the really poor will not receive as much as they would under Reverse Tax.

It is now well known, for instance, that many council houses are occupied by families who, though they may have had lower incomes at the time when they obtained them, now enjoy incomes higher than those of many families paying unsubsidised rents and in addition rates and taxes to support council-house tenants. A representative sample of 7,203 households, interviewed for the official *Family Expenditure Survey 1975*, showed the distribution summarised in Table II.

TABLE II

HOUSEHOLD INCOME BY TENURE, 1975

	Under £25	£25–50	£50–70	£70–100	Over £100	Total
Owner-occupiers	321	576	637	977	1,112	3,619
Council-house tenants	508	477	454	484	365	2,288
Other tenancies	315	329	252	235	165	1,296

The numbers of relatively well-off families in council houses and of poor families privately renting are alike remarkable.

Council-house rents are subject to partial means-testing. Besides the two major schemes of Supplementary Benefits and FIS there are, indeed, now no less than 44 separate lesser means-tested benefits provided from public funds (panel, pp. 28–29). This number is now to be augmented by a further

[27]

STATE MEANS-TESTED BENEFITS

I. BENEFITS ADMINISTERED BY
CENTRAL GOVERNMENT DEPARTMENTS

(a) *Statutory assessments*	*Administering Authority*
1. Free welfare foods (milk and vitamins)	Department of Health and Social Security and Welsh Office
2. Relief from National Health Service charges: Dental and optical charges Charges for prescriptions and elastic hosiery Charges for wigs and fabric supports	Department of Health and Social Security and Welsh Office
3. Patients' hospital travelling expenses	Department of Health and Social Security and Welsh Office
4. Legal aid (civil)	The Lord Chancellor's Department. Scottish Home and Health Department
5. Legal aid (civil claims not involving proceedings)	The Law Societies
6. Legal advice	The Law Societies
7. Legal aid (criminal)	The courts (under the guidance of the Home Department)
8. Remission of direct grant school tuition fees (England and Wales)	Schools on behalf of the Department of Education and Science and Welsh Education Office
9. Training allowances for young people unable to get suitable training or progressive employment in their own areas	Department of Employment
10. Professional training scheme for the disabled	Department of Employment
11. Grants to registered disabled people for special aids for employment, excessive travel to work expenses or for starting a small business	Department of Employment
12. Higher education awards for attending first degree or comparable courses (Scotland)	Scottish Education Department
(b) *Discretionary assessments*	
13. Higher education awards for post-graduate or similar courses	Various central government departments and agencies

II. BENEFITS ADMINISTERED BY LOCAL AUTHORITIES

(a) *Statutory assessments*

14. Rate rebates
15. Free school meals
16. Higher education awards for students attending designated courses at first degree and comparable level
17. Residential accommodation for the elderly or handicapped
18. Temporary accommodation for homeless persons
19. Rent rebates and rent allowances

(b) *Discretionary assessments*

20. Further education awards for students attending non-designated courses
21. Awards for non-advanced further education courses (Scotland)
22. Clothing for children at school unable to take full advantage of the education because of inadequacy or unsuitability of clothing
23. School clothing and uniform grants
24. Educational maintenance allowances (higher school bursaries in Scotland) for school pupils over the statutory minimum leaving age
25. Boarding education allowances. (In Scotland the Central Bursaries Scheme, administered by the Scottish Education Department, makes allowances to pupils who have no residential qualifications for a grant from a local authority.)
26. Independent day school fees
27. Services for children in care
28. Residential accommodation for mothers and babies
29. Day nurseries
30. Residential accommodation for adults mentally disordered
31. Meals in centres for the mentally disordered, elderly or handicapped
32. Meals on wheels
33. Recreational facilities and occupational centres for the elderly or handicapped
34. Personal aids and equipment for the handicapped
35. Adaptation of houses
36. Home helps
37. Chiropody
38. Recuperative holidays and convalescence
39. Nutrients, foods, etc. certified for medical purposes
40. Family planning
41. Loan of nursing equipment
42. Assistance in kind or in emergency in cash where necessary to promote the welfare of children by diminishing the need to receive them in care

Scotland only

43. Local authority social work assistance in kind where assistance in other form would cause higher expense to the local authority
44. Local authority social work assistance in cash in an emergency where higher expense would otherwise be caused to the local authority

Source: Minutes of Evidence by Dept. of Health and Social Security and Board of Inland Revenue, *Select Committee on Tax Credits 1972-73.* 8 February 1973: HC 64–iv, HMSO, 1973, pp. 47–48.

means-tested fund to relieve those who are judged too poor to pay their electricity accounts.

III. THE PRINCIPLE

Reverse Tax: three modifications

The simple idea of paying 'Reverse Tax' to every family whose assessed income fell below a reasonably based minimum must be modified in three respects.

(i) *Proof of claim*

Firstly, it would not suffice for the person or family claiming Reverse Tax simply to demonstrate that they lacked income— they would have to demonstrate the reason: unemployment, sickness, regular but low earnings, or other. These claims would have to be checked through something like the present procedures of doctors' certificates and occasional inspector's visits in sickness claims, and in the case of unemployment claims, availability for work, including routine signing-on at labour exchanges, with a requirement, after a specified number of weeks of benefit, to take any available work offered, even if lower paid than the applicant's customary trade. It would be necessary to make the firm decision that refusal of such employment (or nominal acceptance followed by early subsequent dismissal) would invalidate the claim to Reverse Tax.

The work test would have to be imposed after, say, 13 weeks of unemployment (the present period: but recent disclosures suggest it is far from so in practice). It would be intolerable to have able-bodied people living permanently on Reverse Tax payments—and devoting their principal energies to asking for more. While the applicant would be required to take work in any trade of which he was capable, he should not be compelled to leave his home and family. This provision would of course raise difficulties in economically depressed regions. Men should not be encouraged to go where no work is available. A man whose home had always been in a Welsh valley would have a fair claim, but not the 'hippie' who had migrated there. There should be no compulsion, but assistance should be offered in cases where the family was willing to move to a place where employment was available.

It is sometimes suggested that such offers of employment should be work 'suitable to the individual'. The adoption of this principle would be a step on the slippery slope—some individuals consider almost no work suitable for them. On the other hand, the criterion should be that the person concerned should not be asked to take work clearly beyond his physical or mental capacity.

The administration (stricter than at present) would undoubtedly be a disagreeable task for the civil servants. Their decision should not be without appeal. The aptly named office of 'Umpire' provided in the old Unemployment Insurance Act should be resuscitated. The holders of such office should have judicial status, and be independent of the executive authority.

Many employers now, both of non-manual and of manual workers, continue paying salaries or wages, at any rate for illnesses of limited duration. It is possible that either by custom or by law this practice will be extended, in which event, of course, claims for Reverse Tax will be much reduced.

(ii) *Immediate help*

Secondly, need is usually immediate—certainly families could not be expected to wait for their final assessment after the end of the tax year. Assessment of family income on a weekly basis would cause high administrative costs and difficulties. The procedure therefore should be that any family applying for Reverse Tax, on valid grounds as indicated above, could receive it immediately, subject to an upper limit of 70 per cent of the relevant unskilled wage (male, female or juvenile) receivable by the applicant, on the grounds of unemployment or sickness.[1]

The assessment of these minimum wage standards would constitute a task for administrators. They might differ regionally, and vary from time to time with labour market conditions. At the end of the tax year, however, all such Reverse Tax payments received should be brought into account and related to the year's total income. In some cases, they would have to be supplemented: in others repayments would have to be made, mostly by additions to the subsequent year's normal weekly deductions made by employers. (There would be difficulties with people with no employer in the following year.) To dis-

---

[1] The applicant would be entitled to receive up to this limit irrespective of wife's earnings or other subsidiary family income. If the number of dependants were such that (any subsidiary family income being taken into account) the applicant, in regular work at the unskilled wage, were able to claim Reverse Tax, the Reverse Tax should also be payable to him during unemployment or illness.

courage comparatively wealthy families from trying their hand at applying temporarily for Reverse Tax benefits, provision should be made that if, at the end of the tax year, income was found to be far above the minimum taxable limit, the Reverse Tax received would have to be repaid together with a substantial penalty.

Besides current earnings, income from property or other sources would be taken into account. The claimant would not, however, be required to sell part or all of his property before claiming benefit. For the aged (below), a partial sale of property is proposed.

For owner-occupiers of houses or apartments the 'imputed income' (expected gross rent obtainable from letting the property, less rates, maintenance expenses, insurance, etc, and also interest on a mortgage) should be taken into account. Otherwise we should be giving owner-occupying families an advantage over tenants.

(iii) *Family, not personal, income base*
Thirdly, a more fundamental change is that tax would have to be assessed, and Reverse Tax paid (the same methods must of necessity be used for both) according to family rather than personal income. A person who is unemployed or ill may need temporary help, but much less if other members of the family are at work earning good wages. And the Reverse Tax system would quickly break down if all those who work only occasionally (including, for example, student sons of wealthy families who work during vacations) were thereafter able to go on claiming that they had lost their incomes, and required support. The word 'family' would require precise definition for taxation purposes. It would include married people unless judicially separated, and all children or adults dependent on them.

Young persons could be separated from their parents' families for tax purposes on their own option at any time after the age of 18. Temporary co-habitation would not constitute 'family'. Married couples would generally be freed from mutual financial obligations only on judicial separation, without maintenance orders; though sometimes *de facto* complete separation might have to be treated as *de jure*.

Instead of reductions or rebates for dependants, etc., it is proposed that, for tax purposes, the income of all the 'family' (as defined above) should be aggregated, then divided by a figure based on, but not necessarily identical with, the number in the family (below). It will be objected that such a measure will mainly benefit higher-income families with dependants. It should. Consider two successful business or professional men, living side by side, and earning the same income. One has only a dependent wife, the other is a widower with a number of children and an infirm elderly relative to provide for. It is clear there is a wide difference between their justly-assessed abilities to pay taxation, much more than that now provided by the small dependants' allowances.

Family income 'unit' system and proposed scales

The divisors to be applied to aggregated family income, to allow for family size, should not be crudely based on numbers in the family. To provide a given standard of well-being for two people does not cost twice as much as for one, nor for four people twice as much as for two. The system of units proposed is to treat a married couple without dependants as one unit, and each additional person in the family as one-quarter of a unit (i.e. a family of six would count as two units). Single-person families would count as five-eighths of a unit, i.e. the cost of providing a given standard of living for one person is estimated at rather over half that for a married couple. Single-parent families would be allowed one-eighth of a unit additional to those indicated by the numbers in the family. This would assist them in obtaining Reverse Tax, or reduce their income-tax liability.

The scales proposed give results similar (though a little more generous to large families) to those obtained in a scientific inquiry into the amounts of expenditure required to maintain welfare equivalence of families of different size.[1]

	Family size					
	2	3	4	5	6	7
Scales proposed	1	1.25	1.5	1.75	2	2.25
Seneca-Taussig scale	1	1.25	1.46	1.67	1.88	2.11

These scales, however, take account only of cash expenditure. Repugnant though many mothers would find the idea that

---

[1] Joseph J. Seneca and Michael K. Taussig, 'Family Equivalence Scales and Personal Income Tax Exemptions for Children', *Review of Economics and Statistics*, August 1971.

[33]

they might be 'paid' for bringing up their children, it is nevertheless true that the 'cost' of a young child would be much higher if we took account of all the unpaid work a mother does for it—whether or not she wished to devote her time to paid or unpaid work elsewhere.

Reverse Tax would therefore be paid and income tax assessed on family income per 'unit'.

It would be necessary to provide that Reverse Tax payments would be legally receivable by the head of the family, just as he or she would be legally liable for the payment of the tax on the incomes of other members of the 'family' defined for tax purposes, as a male head is now for his wife's.

Those (regrettably, perhaps many) who will say that the unit divisor system is neither practicable nor desirable are revealing their insularity. French income tax law (which incidentally does not levy more than 60 per cent of each additional franc earned, even at the highest income levels) provides as follows:

'For taxpayers other than single persons, the taxable income is divided by application of the following numbers (family co-efficients):

1.0	Single, divorced or widowed with no child
1.5	Single, divorced or widowed under certain circumstances with no present dependant
2.0	Married without dependent child; single or divorced with one dependent child
2.5	Married or widowed with one dependent child; single or divorced with two dependent children
3.0	Married or widowed with two dependent children; single or divorced with three dependent children
3.5	Married or widowed with three dependent children; single or divorced with four dependent children
4.0	Married or widowed with four dependent children; single or divorced with five dependent children

and so on, each additional child taken into account for 0.5.

Disabled children (minors or of age), holders of the invalidity card, entitled to an additional half point.

A supplementary point is granted to couples when each spouse is disabled.'

For a disabled couple without a dependent child, for example, the divisor would rise from 2.0 to 3.0. The French system does not, however, provide for adult dependants (except for the disabled), as is proposed here.

IV. THE PROPOSAL

The figures which follow, regarding both benefits and estimated costs, are intended to refer to the first half of 1977. In the light of recent trends of average earnings, it is assumed that by this time earnings will be 25 per cent above the annual average for 1975, income distribution remaining unchanged. Anyone wishing to make the comparison more precise may say that these results refer, not to any specified date, but to the time when average earnings have risen to 25 per cent above their 1975 level (which will probably be sometime in the first half of 1977).

The rate of 'cut-out'

As other income received rises, Reverse Tax must necessarily 'cut-out'. The only question is the rate at which 'cut-out' is to take place. If Reverse Tax simply supplements income, i.e. it goes down by £1 for each £1 that income rises, a 100 per cent 'cut-out', it may be expected to have an extremely damaging effect on the incentive to earn, or to conserve income-earning property. Extremely high rates of 'cut-out' of social benefits in effect apply to many families at the present time; and it is indeed surprising that more low-earning families have not stopped working.

The decision about the permissible 'cut-out' rate constitutes a problem of the first order. As with other social and economic problems, we may attempt to solve it by systematic observations and analytical reasoning, tempered by common sense. It is, however, rare that any social or economic problem has been submitted to experiment, in the sense that scientists use this word, i.e. the deliberate creation of specified external conditions with a view to observing their consequences. Any 'experiment' on a social problem must inevitably be far more laborious, slow and costly than an experiment in a laboratory (costly though many of the latter are now becoming).

The New Jersey experiment

A long and costly experiment, commonly known as the 'New Jersey Experiment', was financed by the US Government, in order to throw light on precisely this problem, namely the effects of various income maintenance proposals, with varying 'cut-out' rates, on incentives to earn.[1] It covered a large number of lower-income families, both white and black, in industrial towns in New Jersey. If the effects on incentives are to be properly gauged, an experiment has to run over a considerable period. Unfortunately the New Jersey State Government, in the middle of the experiment, introduced a new system of welfare payments which, however welcome in itself, made the interpretation of the experimental results more difficult.

The principal 'cut-out' rates examined were of 50 and 70 per cent, i.e. 50 cents and 70 cents respectively of benefit withdrawn for each additional dollar earned. It soon became clear that any lower cut-out rate had little significant effect on incentive. This also appeared to be true of the 50 per cent cut-out rate. That a 70 per cent cut-out rate would also have little significant effect on incentive appeared probable, though the evidence was less clear.

A 70 per cent cut-out rate is included in the proposals below, for reasons indicated.

Some say it will obviously be regarded as unjust and destructive of incentive that a family receiving Reverse Tax should lose 70 per cent of any additional sum they earn. Others reply that present effective cut-out rates on many poor families are in the neighbourhood of 100 per cent, sometimes even exceeding 100 per cent, which so far appear to have had little disincentive effect. But the 70 per cent cut-out rate is a regrettable necessity. It is to be hoped that it is the optimum compromise between minimising the tax cost and avoiding serious disincentive effects.

There may also be some complaints about the supposed comparison between the 50 per cent maximum marginal rate of taxation proposed for higher incomes and the 70 per cent tax on additional earnings of low-income families. But people

---

[1] The full report, *Final Report of the New Jersey Graduated Work Incentive Experiment*, was published in 1973 and 1974 by University of Wisconsin Institute for Research on Poverty, and by Mathematica, Princeton. A commentary on the findings is given in Joseph Pechman and Michael Timpane (eds.), *Work Incentives and Income Guarantees*, Brookings Institution, Washington DC, 1975. A useful preliminary summary was published in *Scientific American*, October 1972. This journal justified its entry into a field remote from its usual subject-matter by its desire to welcome what it described as the first large-scale use of 'experiment' applied to a social problem.

who reason in this manner do not see the fundamental difference between a tax imposed on a person's own earnings and a partial withdrawal of benefit from those claiming to live on other people's earnings.

Desirable objectives irreconcilable

The designer of a system of Reverse Taxation is bound by certain unavoidable arithmetical imperatives. If we were free to choose, we would have a high rate of payment to families with little or no income, a low cut-out rate for anything additional which they earned, while at the same time not designing a scheme which cost too much, or which applied to too large a proportion of the population.

These objectives are irreconcilable. If we wish to pay, at supposed 1977 earnings and prices, £25 per week to a married couple with no dependants, described as one 'unit', with no other income, with a cut-out rate of 50 per cent, the 'base' income (below which Reverse Tax is payable, and only above which ordinary income tax becomes payable) must be as high as £50 per unit. But if we adopt this 'base' income we will find we are paying Reverse Tax to a third of the entire population, or about 6 million families, to be met (together with all other expenses of government) out of taxation paid by the remaining two-thirds, or about 12 million.

The distribution of incomes per 'unit' (excluding social security benefits) in 1975 is shown in Chart B. There is a clear break in the distribution at about £25 per week per 'unit' in 1975 (£31.25 at supposed 1977 rate of earnings). Below this figure are to be found some 18 per cent of the population (almost half of them retirement pensioners). To raise the figure to £30 (£37.50 at 1977 earnings) would increase the proportion of the population covered to 23 per cent. These increases in the proportion covered become still more rapid as we go up the income scale, as is shown by Chart B. Common sense tells us that, even at 23 per cent, we would be trying to include under Reverse Tax payments (and to exempt from income tax) too high a proportion of the population.

'Base' income £31.25 per family 'unit' in 1977: Reverse Tax £21.88

The 'base' income below which reverse tax is to be payable is thus taken at £31.25 per week per 'unit' at supposed 1977

[37]

rates of earning (corresponding to £25 in 1975). With the cut-out rate of 70 per cent this will give £21.88 per 'unit' (at 1977 rates) to a married couple with no other income. This will apply to those temporarily lacking income through unemployment, illness, business reverses, etc., and to families whose current earnings fall short of needs per 'unit' so defined.

Aged and retired: choice between present and new schemes of Reverse Tax and indexed annuity

The aged and retired would have the same right as others to apply for Reverse Tax on the grounds of inadequate or no income. In addition a new system of annuities, with price-indexed benefits, is proposed for the aged. They would then have the option of choosing the new scheme or their present pensions plus supplementary benefits, etc., whichever they found more advantageous.

The payments proposed will, however, fall short of those now received by the aged who (from November 1976) are receiving £24.50 for a married couple and £15.30 for a single person together with, in many cases, rent, rates and other supplementary benefits. (The present scale for a single pensioner is five-eighths of that for a married couple, exactly the ratio used in the scheme of 'units' proposed above.)

It is proposed that the aged with little or no income, like others, should apply for Reverse Tax, subject to income tests. In addition they should be enabled to purchase, in most cases provided with, an annuity of £7.50 per person per week, this amount to rise with any subsequent rise in prices.

So old people would be able to claim support in two forms: firstly, an income support, which right they would share with others lacking income, rising to a maximum of £21.88 (at 1977 earnings) for a married couple without dependants; and, secondly, a life annuity contractually indexed to changes in

---

DEFINITION OF 'UNITS' (CHART B)★

Number in family	Units
1	.625
2	1
3	1.25
4	1.5
5	1.75

etc.

(Single-parent families allowed additional .125 units)

[38]

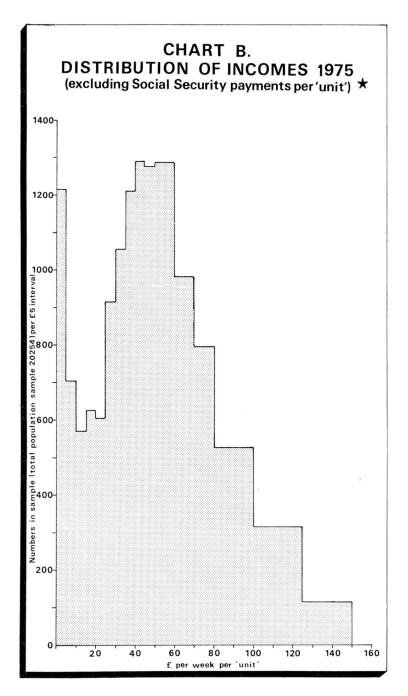

CHART B.
DISTRIBUTION OF INCOMES 1975
(excluding Social Security payments per 'unit') ★

Numbers in sample (total population sample 20254) per £5 interval

£ per week per 'unit'

[39]

prices. It is expected that the income support would also be periodically adjusted by legislation as prices and incomes changed, though at present no contractual obligation is proposed.

The reason for proposing this separation is to take account in the first place of people over 65 who have substantial earnings or other income and who, therefore, at any rate while it lasts, should not claim income support.

The annuity proposal is meant to take account of old people with substantial property, because property would not be taken into account in Reverse Tax assessment, either for young or for old. Old people who possessed substantial property would be given the opportunity of purchasing, from their own resources, the same annuities, indexed for price changes. Those possessing a small amount of property would have part of the cost of the annuity provided for them. Calculations are made for a 50 per cent cut-out rate. Thus if the annuity cost £3,000 (in 'indexed' money) for an applicant possessing £2,000, the applicant would be expected to find £1,000 of the cost, and the state would find the remainder.

The claimant would not be compelled to sell his property, but could retain some or all of it. In the extreme case of a married couple possessing substantial property, and therefore ineligible for state support, deciding to retain all their property, and not purchase an indexed annuity, they would be free to do so. If they lost their property and the income from it they would have no claim to an annuity, and would have to live on £21.88 per week (or any amended amount) of income support.

The principal form of property held by most old people is a dwelling house, often much larger than they need. If they could be persuaded to sell these houses, and to live in smaller apartments, they would considerably relieve the shortage of housing now felt keenly by younger families. They should not be *compelled* to do so. But they should not complain about, or expect relief from, rates or other taxation falling upon the occupation of houses, which may not be an ideal form of taxation, but which do at any rate have the merit of discouraging wasteful use of housing space.

Annuities administered via insurance companies

The indexed annuities should be administered through insurance companies as intermediaries. Having obtained a certified valuation of his property (with penalties for mis-statement), the applicant would seek an indexed annuity from an insurance company. The state would supply to the insurance company indexed bonds corresponding to the actuarial valuation of the applicant's expectation of life. If the applicant had no property the state would provide the whole amount. To the extent that the applicant possessed property, the state would charge the insurance company the face value of part or all of the indexed bonds issued, and the insurance company in turn would recover this amount from the applicant. If there were difficulties about the applicant immediately disposing of 50 per cent of his property for cash, it could be handed over to the insurance company for temporary administration.

People who, even with the income support and the annuity combined, would still be worse off than they are under present arrangements, should be given the opportunity of continuing to receive what they do at present. They would consist of some families with high incomes or property, receiving old-age pensions, which they regard as a contributory contractual right; and some receiving unusually large supplementary benefits.

Yield from new tax scales

The expected yields from various possible scales of income tax under the revised conditions, i.e. with minimum 'base', below which reverse tax would be payable, are shown in Table III. The proposed new tax scales are to replace income tax and also employees' National Insurance contributions, both of which at present may fall on families well below the poverty line. They show assessments to be made on families per 'unit'.

Even at low levels many earners now are in effect faced with a 40 per cent marginal tax rate (employees' contribution to National Insurance included). While it is not possible to measure, this must have a strong deterrent effect on incentive. The tax scales calculated in Table III show the possibility of lower marginal rates over at any rate a considerable part of the income range. The 70 per cent cut-out rate for people receiving reverse taxes, however, is a regrettable necessity.

The progression from the initial tax rate to the 50 per cent maximum can be on various possible scales. Their incidence on typical incomes is shown in Tables III and IV, together with their expected yields. These scales are designed to advance smoothly (in a hyperbolic relationship)[1] towards the maximum of 50 per cent, and to avoid the awkward and sometimes inequitable jolts in present tax scales.

Comparisons are shown with the rates imposable under present income tax and National Insurance law. Besides the exemption of obviously needy families, and the limitation of the maximum marginal rate to 50 per cent, for most incomes both average and marginal rates of tax will be considerably lower than they are now.

TABLE III

REVERSE TAX: PROPOSED TAX SCALES

Percentage rate of tax y on income above taxable minimum x
(Incomes expressed in £ per week per 'unit')

	Expected *1977* yield *£ billion*
Initial tax rate 20 per cent	
Scale A $y = 20 + 30 \, x/(x + 150)$	16.2
Scale B $y = 20 + 30 \, x/(x + 100)$	17.7
Scale C $y = 20 + 30 \, x/(x + 50)$	18.7
Initial tax rate 25 per cent	
Scale D $y = 25 + 25 \, x/(x + 150)$	18.0
Scale E $y = 25 + 25 \, x/(x + 100)$	19.2
Scale F $y = 25 + 25 \, x/(x + 50)$	20.1
Initial tax rate 30 per cent	
Scale G $y = 30 + 20 \, x/(x + 150)$	19.7
Scale H $y = 30 + 20 \, x/(x + 100)$	20.4
Scale I $y = 30 + 20 \, x/(x + 50)$	21.4

For example, under Scale A a married couple without children (i.e. one unit) with a weekly income of £60 would be assessed on the amount by which this exceeded the 'base' income of £31.25, i.e. on £28.75, which becomes x in the equation. So $(x + 150)$ becomes 178.75 and $x/(x + 150)$ becomes .1608. This is multiplied by 30 to give 4.824, which is added to 20 to give 24.824 as the percentage rate of taxation on the assessment of £28.75, i.e. £7.14 tax.

A married couple with four dependent children (i.e. two units) would likewise be assessed on the amount by which their income exceeded *two* basic incomes, i.e. £62.50; and if they were receiving less income they would be entitled to Reverse Tax.

When x is near zero (i.e. just above the taxable minimum)

---

[1] The hyperbola is the most convenient mathematical expression for a relationship rising progressively towards a maximum (asymptote), but never exceeding it. Its equation can be written in various degrees of generality. The simple form used here is $y = ax/(x + b)$ in which, it is seen, y gradually approaches the value a as x becomes larger.

TABLE IV

TAX PAYABLE OR REVERSE TAX (+) RECEIVABLE ON LOWEST, MEDIAN AND MAXIMUM SCALES, COMPARED WITH PRESENT INCOME TAX PLUS EMPLOYEE'S NI CONTRIBUTIONS

| | Weekly Income £ | | | | | | | | | |
	30	40	50	60	80	100	125	150	175	200
				(£ per week per household)						
Scale A										
Single person	2.4	5.2	8.3	11.8	25.3	35.0	48.5	62.2	75.9	89.7
Married couple	+0.9	1.9	4.4	7.1	13.3	20.2	38.9	51.2	64.1	77.5
Married couple, 2 dependent children	+11.8	+4.7	0.6	2.8	7.8	13.6	21.6	30.3	39.6	64.2
Married couple, 4 dependent children	+22.7	+15.7	+18.7	+1.8	3.8	8.8	15.6	23.4	31.6	40.4
Scale E										
Single person	3.0	6.4	10.1	14.0	22.6	31.5	43.8	54.7	66.8	78.5
Married couple	+0.9	2.3	5.4	8.8	16.2	24.1	34.7	45.7	56.9	68.6
*Married couple, 2 dependent children	+11.8	+4.7	0.8	3.4	9.8	16.7	26.2	36.1	46.6	57.5
Married couple, 4 dependent children	+22.7	+15.7	+8.7	+1.8	4.6	10.8	19.2	28.4	38.2	48.2
Scale I										
Single person	3.5	7.4	11.6	16.0	24.9	34.1	46.4	58.3	70.7	83.1
Married couple	+0.9	2.8	6.4	10.2	18.5	27.2	38.3	50.3	61.8	74.1
Married couple, 2 dependent children	+11.8	+4.7	0.9	4.2	11.4	19.4	29.9	40.8	52.0	63.5
Married couple, 4 dependent children	+22.7	+15.7	+8.7	+1.8	5.6	12.8	22.4	32.6	43.4	54.4
Present income tax plus employee's National Insurance[1]										
Single person	7.2	11.4	15.5	19.6	27.7	35.6	46.3	58.6	72.7	87.7
Married couple	6.9	9.0	13.1	17.2	25.3	33.2	43.2	55.2	68.7	87.3
*Married couple, 2 dependent children	1.7	5.0	9.1	13.2	21.3	29.2	38.2	49.4	62.3	76.7
Married couple, 4 dependent children	1.7	2.3	5.0	9.1	17.2	25.1	33.9	44.1	56.1	69.8

* These figures were used to construct the chart on the front cover.
[1] Present income tax refers to 1976–77 rates,

these rates (on the amount of income above the taxable minimum) become approximately 20, 25 and 30 per cent respectively. When x is large all rates gradually approach, but never exceed, the proposed maximum rate of 50 per cent. Taxes payable are shown for Scales A (lowest), E (medium) and I (maximum).

Table IV shows, for three representative tax scales, the proposed income tax payable, or Reverse Tax receivable, for different family compositions and income levels, in comparison with the income tax plus employees' National Insurance contributions payable by them now.

The maximum rate

The proposed maximum rate of tax, even on the highest income, is 50 per cent. Common sense and the experience of other countries alike indicate that the present maximum rates are inherently absurd, leading some of the most successful business and professional men to 'opt out' and to retire prematurely, or to live abroad, and to people at every level of income devoting much of their energies (which should be used to better purpose) to attempts to avoid tax by legal or semi-legal means.

The principle of 'equality of sacrifice' also leads to a similar conclusion. Many economists hold that in general, though it cannot be claimed as a universal truth, that the loss of economic welfare caused by each £ of taxation is much less for a rich family than for a middle-income or poor family—but not to a limitless extent. An approximate measurement of this loss of economic welfare at differing income levels is made in my article 'The Marginal Utility of Income'.[1] It can be deduced that a tax of 50 per cent on high incomes represents about the same sacrifice of economic welfare as the 25 per cent now imposed on poor families, principally through various forms of indirect taxation.

No doubt objection will be made to the division of family income by the number of 'units' in the family, in the case of higher-income earners with a number of dependants, on the

---

[1] *Oxford Economic Papers*, July 1973. A simple method of analysis is to compare the amounts of money which people at different income levels are willing to spend in order to save one hour's travel time, treated as an objective measure of utility. This gives results in accordance with more refined analyses of consumption expenditures at different income levels.

ground that higher allowances for each child are 'given' to higher-income families than to lower-income families. Anyone who reasons in this manner is basing himself on the fundamentally false, and indeed dangerous, premise that all property and income implicitly belongs to the state, which then proceeds to 'give' to each family an after-tax income it considers appropriate. This is not a matter of the state 'giving', but of its refraining from imposing unjust taxation on families whose ability to pay, on any rational measurement, is clearly much less than that of families enjoying the same income with fewer dependants.

Working wives: increased incentive to look after family

Every married woman must decide for herself whether she will seek outside employment, or stay at home to care for her children. At present all the economic incentives are unbalanced in favour of working for 'gain'. Consider a married couple with two children under 11, the husband earning £2,500 and the wife capable of earning £1,500. Under present tax and national insurance legislation, her work would add a little under £1,200 net to the family income. Under our proposals, the £2,500 income would be on the border line for receiving Reverse Tax, while the £4,000 would be subject to income tax at a rate of £8–£11 per week according to the scale chosen, thus reducing the wife's net contribution to about £1,000. In view of the effort involved, the children's loss of their mother's attention, the additional costs (travel, clothing, meals, etc.) incurred by the mother working, and also some increase in household costs, the incentive to stay at home is much augmented.

Surcharge on investment income

The surcharge on investment incomes should be abolished. Apart from the allowance for family needs, tax-deductibility should be confined to expenses necessarily incurred in earning the income. Generally speaking, tax-deductibility is not the best way of encouraging particular forms of outlay—for the good reason that, with a progressive tax scale, such concessions are much more valuable to a rich than to a poor taxpayer. If the government has good grounds for encouraging any form of activity it should do so by means of a subsidy or voucher

[45]

earmarked for that purpose, not by tax concessions of unequal incidence.

Tax encouragement for charitable giving

The only exceptions to this rule should be for donations to charitable or related organisations, where it is indeed desirable to encourage the rich to give more than the poor.

The removal of tax-deductibility under these various concessions should, however, be phased gradually rather than peremptorily.

Taxing investment income twice

The argument for taxing investment income more highly than 'earned' income goes back to Dilke's proposals to the Liberal Government in 1906. But economic theory disagrees. In Pigou's *A Study of Public Finance*[1] it was clearly shown that to tax the income from which savings are made and then to tax the revenue from them was, in effect, taxing savings twice.

In any event, it becomes impossible to distinguish the two elements in the case of a man actively running a business in which he has invested considerable capital.

Tax refunds on mortgage interest

Tax deductibility of mortgage interest on dwellings is justifiable only if the 'imputed income' from the house is regarded as taxable, as is proposed above for Reverse Tax claimants, and as used to be the case under Schedule A of the Income Tax Act. The effects of the abolition of Schedule A, and the granting of tax deductibility for mortgage interest, have been to increase demand and to raise the price of houses—which is welcome news to people who own their homes, but not to the minority, largely of poorer people, who do not.

To grant tax deductibility for costs of daily travel to and from work, as is now being demanded, would have the effect of encouraging people to live further away from their work than they otherwise would, and of raising the prices of houses and land in the remoter suburbs.

[1] Macmillan, 1928 (3rd edn., 1947).

The final amount of Reverse Tax payable, to be adjusted at
the end of the year, will be seven-tenths of the amount by
which the year's 'per unit' income falls short of the base, or
minimum taxable, income.

Consider now a family dependent on a man earning £60 per
week, with the divisor for family size of 1.5. He is unemployed
or ill for 15 weeks, and applies for Reverse Tax. He is advised
that the maximum he can receive in any week is £35 (seven-
tenths of unskilled wage of £50), but that this will be entered
on his tax record, and a final adjustment made at the end of
the year. Assume he applies for £30 for each week when he is
ill or unemployed, a total of £450. At the end of the year his
earnings for 37 weeks are assessed at £2,220, as against the
'base' figure at which Reverse Tax is to end and income tax is
to begin of £31.25 per unit per week (multiplied by 1.5 for
family size, and 52.14 weeks, to £2,444 annually). The
difference between his income and this figure is £224. So he is
entitled to seven-tenths of this amount, or £157, as against the
£375 he has received. He will thus have to repay £218.
Against this, however, he will be due for a refund of some
income tax paid on his behalf by his employer during the past
year.

Alternatively, let us assume that he suffers 20 weeks unemployment or illness, of which the first 10 are met from his own
savings, and the next 10 by Reverse Tax at £20 per week, or
£200 in all. In this case his annual earnings of £1,920, com-
pared with the standard of £2,444, leave a difference of £524.
Seven-tenths of this is £367, as against the £200 he has
received. He will therefore receive an additional £167, besides
refund of income tax paid.

But, again, consider such a family in which the wife is in
regular employment, earning £30 per week. The husband will
still be entitled to apply for assistance up to £35 per week
while ill or unemployed; but with a total family income (in
both examples) well above the taxable minimum, this would
all have to be repaid.

Reverse Tax payments, which at the end of the year either
will be proved justifiable, or be repayable, will not be subject
to income tax at the time they are received.

In deciding how much (if any) to apply for during periods

[47]

TABLE V

EXAMPLES OF PRESENT AND PROPOSED INCOME AND TAX UNDER
REVERSE TAX FOR PEOPLE ILL OR UNEMPLOYED FOR 10 WEEKS
(MEDIAN TAX SCALE)

	Earnings or former earnings £/week	'Units'	'Basic' Income £/week[a]	Proposed income tax (Scale E) or Reverse Tax (+ sign) £/week[b]	Net family spending power £/week when working (after tax, rent, rates, etc.) Proposed	Present
Single man	45	.625	19.53	8.5	29.2	24.4
	55			12.6	35.1	30.3
	75			21.1	46.6	42.1
	95			30.2	57.5	54.0
Married couple, no children	45	1	31.25	4.2	33.5	27.2
	55			7.8	39.9	32.6
	75			16.1	51.6	44.5
	95			24.8	62.9	56.3
Married couple, one child aged 3	45	1.25	39.06	1.6	35.3	30.8
	55			4.9	42.0	33.9
	75			12.8	54.1	45.7
	95			21.4	65.5	57.5
Married couple, two children aged 4 and 6	45	1.5	46.88	+1.3	37.9	34.9
	55			2.3	44.3	37.2
	75			9.5	57.1	48.0
	95			17.9	68.7	59.9
Married couple, four children aged 3, 8, 11 and 16	45	2	62.5	+12.3	48.0	45.3
	55			+5.3	51.0	46.7
	75			3.7	62.0	53.1
	95			11.3	74.4	64.9

[a] Below which Reverse Tax receivable and above which income tax payable.
[b] National Insurance employees' contributions abolished.
[c] Work expenses assumed £1.75 per week, rent and rates as shown in Chart A (table, for of p. 18). Present figure takes into account income tax, National Insurance, family allowances, family income supplementation, rent and rate rebates, free school meals and welfare milk. Present income tax refers to 1976–77 rates.

of illness or unemployment, families will have to make their own estimates of how long such needs are likely to last, and of what their year-end income is likely to be.

Penalty rates

If a family income per 'unit' of £31.25 per week is to be the minimum below which Reverse Tax would be payable, and if average income received at the end of the year worked out above this level, some repayment of any Reverse Tax received during the year would be required. This rule would prevail up

TABLE V (*continued*)

Net family spending (lower £/week when not working after tax, rent, rates, etc.) Present^d £	Maximum immediate grants payable for 10 weeks' unemployment or illness^e £	Do. less rent and rates £	Of which repayable^f £	Repayable at penalty rates^g £	Additional Reverse Tax receivable during year £
19.2	280	225		325	
20.1	280	225		398	
20.9	280	225		543	
20.9	280	225		685	
27.8	280	225	280		
28.6	280	225	280		
29.5	280	225		338	
29.5	280	225		429	
31.2	280	217	176		
32.8	280	217	280		
33.6	280	217	280		
33.6	280	217		343	
33.9	328	262			52
37.2	328	262	248		
38.0	328	262	328		
38.0	328	262		337	
41.5	438	362			530
46.1	438	362			227
46.6	438	362	361		
46.6	438	362	438		

Without taking into account tax refunds which in many cases make the amount receivable when unemployed considerably larger (table, p. 20).
I.e. 70 per cent of assumed unskilled wage of £40, supplemented for numbers of children.
If earnings for remainder of year are as specified.
Unless repayment is made immediately after resumption of work.

to a per 'unit' income received from other sources of, say, £50. Above that, penalty rates of repayment would apply, because it will be necessary to discourage high-income families from trying their luck at getting a free loan of Reverse Tax during temporary illness or unemployment. The amount to be repaid should be set at such Reverse Tax received multiplied by the proportion by which per head income received during the year (excluding any Reverse Tax payment) exceeded, in this case, £50 per week. For a family whose per 'unit' income at the end of the year was, for instance, ascertained at £75 per week, any Reverse Tax payments received during the year should be

[49]

recovered, at a rate increased by 50 per cent. The penalty would be remitted where the family had made a genuine misjudgement, and made immediate repayment.

Table V shows the combined effects of proposed Reverse Tax payments[1] and one of the new income tax scales (Scale E, at about the middle of the range) on different types of families at different income levels, at work or unemployed, in comparison with the present state of affairs.

The cardinal principle which has to be observed is that the man at work must be substantially better off than the man (for whatever reason) not at work.

Table V makes comparisons of the present and proposed (under the median tax scale E) position of various families in the case of 10 weeks' illness or unemployment. It must be added, however, that after the proposed reforms families would have to make their own provision for many (though not all) of the services listed above (panel, p. 28–9) now provided on a means-tested basis. The comparisons of net family spending power (see also Table V, footnote c) are made after debiting estimated working expenses and rent and rates (whether paid in full or subsidised). Items such as school meals have to be paid for out of net spending power, but in the 'present' columns the subsidy has been included in net spending power.

V. THE COST

The cost of such a scheme is estimated, from information in the *Family Expenditure Survey* (see Appendix), at £3.26 billion per year (Table VI). Present social security payments amounted to £9.6 billion in 1975, a 30 per cent increase on 1974, with every prospect of similar increases in the future. Before we compare these figures, however, the proposed additional payments to the aged must be noted.

Additional payments to old people

Approximate estimation of the cost of these proposals is made below in the light of information about the property holdings of old people shown by Estate Duty statistics.

Those approaching 65 should be given compensation for their legitimate expectations under the contributory scheme,

[1] Calculated in this case on a supposed unskilled wage of £40, i.e. maximum payment (except to larger families) of £28 per week.

TABLE VI

ESTIMATED COST OF REVERSE TAX PROPOSALS, 1977

Data from *Family Expenditure Survey 1975* (7,203 households, 20,254 persons)

Incomes (excluding *Social Security*) per 'unit' (£ per week)

Number of persons	Under 5	5–10	10–15	15–20	20–25	25–30	30–40	40–50	50–60	60–70	70–100	Over 100	Total
Single person (over 65)	475	90	63	40	16	16	36	27	7	6	16	19	811
Single person (under 65)	60	50	45	20	5	20	52	40	39	42	137	120	630
Married couple (man over 65)	440	274	152	80	92	56	68	74	74	38	36	44	1,428
Married couple (man under 65)	24	34	26	36	20	44	132	172	336	252	778	740	2,594
Single-parent families[a]	107	92	71	54	29	36	55	31	15	17	26	3	536
Married couple, one child	9	0	0	27	27	42	114	162	414	384	489	384	2,052
Married couple, two children	12	32	48	84	112	148	636	876	856	492	604	236	4,136
Married couple, three or more children[a]	39	64	98	161	194	341	805	625	356	233	239	136	3,291
All other families[a]	51	71	69	121	111	211	359	549	470	498	1,365	899	4,775
Totals	1,217	707	572	623	606	914	2,257	2,556	2,567	1,962	3,690	2,581	20,253
Estimated cost[b] of Reverse Tax payments 1977 (£ million per year)	1,893	772	278	241	76								3,260

[a] Numbers partly estimated.

[b] Incomes raised by 25 per cent for estimated 1975–77 increase. Reverse Tax allowed of 70 per cent of deficiency below £31.25 per unit base income and numbers raised from sample to national total.

and the right to make advance payments, out of their own savings or property disposals, to purchase the indexed annuities, to come into force at the age of 65, up to the maximum amount under the scheme.

The approximate estimate of the cost of the proposed annuity of £7.50 per week (indexed) for all persons over 65 (males and females pensioned at same age) would be:

(i) *Total cost for people already over 65 in 1977:*
    £21.3 billion indexed 3 per cent bonds of which £5.2 billion would be paid for out of old people's assets (50 per cent cut-out rate) and remainder from government subvention. Bonds to be progressively redeemed over lifetimes of beneficiaries.

(ii) *Cost for people reaching the age of 65 in 1977:*
     An additional bond issue of £2.8 billion would be required, of which about the same proportion as above is expected to be paid for out of the old people's own assets.

In subsequent years no great change is to be expected in the numbers annually reaching 65.

At present it appears necessary to confine the issue of indexed bonds to pensioners, though there are many others also wishing to buy them. These limitations are necessary because it appears that there are considerable difficulties in the way of the immediate issue of large quantities of indexed bonds. For one thing, this would lead to a disastrous fall in the prices of non-indexed bonds. Of the limited quantity which can be issued, first priority in distribution should go to those whose need is greatest.

Besides paying interest, the Government would of course have to repay substantial quantities of these bonds each year to meet the annuitants' claims.

Special provisions

Special provisions will have to be made for the chronically sick and disabled, and this is outside the subject matter of this *Paper*. The same may apply to the genuine permanently unemployable, those needing legal aid (though there may be some abuses here), or those needing retraining. Maintenance of students receiving higher education should in most cases be financed through loans.

Those earning comparatively high incomes who are anxious

about the prospect of unemployment reducing them suddenly to an unaccustomed low level of income should be given every encouragement to organise unemployment insurance among themselves, as did the skilled craftsmen's trade unions in the 19th century.

Administration

For those concerned with administration the question of how the transition could be made to such a scheme is of cardinal importance. Any attempt to make it at one stroke would be administratively unthinkable, quite apart from organised political opposition from those who stood to lose by it.

The following procedure is proposed. Full publicity should first be given to the proposed reduced scales of income tax (with the abolition of employees' National Insurance contributions), the conditions under which Reverse Tax is to be payable (in some cases to be repaid later), and also the right to buy bonds indexed against price increases—the latter with help from public funds for those at or approaching retirement age, but to be permitted also, to a lesser extent, to younger taxpayers.

Once these were well understood, every taxpayer would be allowed to choose between:

(i) Paying income tax and employees' National Insurance contributions at present rates, and retaining all rights as established by present laws and administrative procedures to unemployment, sickness and supplementary benefits, retirement pensions, all other Social Security provisions and means-tested benefits listed above—all such benefits, however, to be taxable.

(ii) Paying income tax at the new reduced rates and renouncing permanently all the rights listed above but with the rights to Reverse Tax and to purchase indexed bonds as described above.

Applicants for unemployment benefits, etc., would have to show tax receipts under Alternative (i) to prove their entitlement.

Renunciation would have to be permanent—a taxpayer who had chosen Alternative (ii) could not revert to Alternative (i).

[53]

In this way, the Inland Revenue would be able to make the change progressively, though as rapidly as possible—it might at some stages be necessary to establish a waiting list for those seeking re-assessment under Alternative (ii).

New taxpayers (including immigrants and school leavers) should all be assessed under Alternative (ii), and have no rights to unemployment benefit, etc.

Advantages and disadvantages

Social workers, now a numerous and organised body, will probably agree that there would be a considerable advantage in these proposals, in contrast to the present state of affairs, in that now many families, for various reasons, are failing to 'take up' the benefits to which they are legally entitled. As disadvantage they will claim—apart from a reduction in the demand for their own services—their conviction that some parents will receive the cash but fail to provide, for example, adequate meals for their children.

A limited amount of such abuse is part of the price which has to be paid for a policy of making people more independent and responsible for their actions. It is relevant to add that in extreme cases of child neglect public authorities have legal rights of intervention.

In any event the general system of social services must not be planned on the basis of rare cases of misuse.

One of the most important elements in the 'poverty trap' is the provision of rent rebates, and their cutting out as incomes increase. The rental market now is completely disorganised, some families paying too much and others too little. The reorganisation of the rental market is a task which has to be undertaken.[1] The mere removal of the regulation which forbids the sub-letting of any part of council houses would itself lead to an increased supply of accommodation at lower rents.

It is recognised, in an obscure way, in official documents that considerable evasion of income tax is now taking place,[2] mainly by small businesses and tradesmen who work almost entirely for cash, and wage-earners employed by them paid in cash. (A firm which keeps true accounts cannot conceal its payments to wage and salary earners.) Considerable additional

[1] F. G. Pennance, *Housing Market Analysis and Policy*, Hobart Paper 48, IEA, 1969.
[2] David R. Morgan, *Over-taxation by Inflation*, Hobart Paper 73, IEA, 1977; and *The State of Taxation*, Readings No. 16, IEA, 1977.

supervision will be required in these cases. Regrettably, this will cause additional administrative expense; but a close check on all wage payments will be necessary if the Reverse Tax system is not to be abused.

At present we must leave open the question whether the entire system of Reverse Taxation should be operated by an enlarged Inland Revenue Department, closing down all other Social Security administration, including that large part of the Department of Employment which is engaged in paying benefits.

Many civil servants will have to be transferred to new duties. If these proposals are confronted with the new spirit of Civil Service union intransigence, objecting to the transfer of civil servants from one employment to another, those concerned should be dismissed. Unlike the position in some trades, there is undoubtedly an over-supply of civil servants.

Proposals are made above on the question whether the transformation should be carried through by gradual phasing, or introduced sharply.

Under the present system of tax administration many people are now exempt from the obligation of making annual tax returns. This obligation will have to be imposed, as it is in other countries.

Should idlers' families suffer?

We still have to face the problem, which indeed also confronted Poor Law officials in the old days, that if relief is to be refused, as indicated above, to the determined idler or 'layabout' or to the striker, what of his family if they make separate application? To this issue, with all its unsatisfactory consequences, there is no satisfactory solution. Other countries' legislation may be noted. In the Netherlands (so far as can be ascertained from documents provided by the Embassy) no provision, and in France only a little municipal provision, is made. In West Germany municipal authorities have powers to make some payment in accordance with their judgement of the circumstances.

PAYE: abolish weekly adjustment

'The PAYE system . . . is complicated and difficult to understand. It requires the employment of some 35,000 staff in the Inland

Revenue and perhaps as many again in industry. It has been found to lack flexibility, and governments—of both political parties—have found it difficult to adapt it to accommodate changes they have found desirable. Nor would those handicaps have been removed even if the system had been operated fully by computers.'[1]

The procedure for adjusting weekly tax deductions for every change of employment (Form P.45) is inordinately costly to administer. It has been stated by one of those principally involved at the time that it arose out of a confused political decision. So far as is known Britain is the only country practising anything like this system. Elsewhere, the usual provision is for all necessary tax adjustments to be made at the end of the tax year. It may be pointed out that the US Internal Revenue Service, with three times as many income taxpayers, employs about the same number of civil servants as the Inland Revenue. The abolition of weekly adjustment should set free sufficient staff to carry out many, if not all, of the other administrative duties required for a Reverse Tax system.

Tax deductions to be made by employers could be fixed on a simple table of dependencies. There is something to be said for fixing these deductions a little on the high side, so that (as in Australia) the average earner receives a tax rebate at the end of the year. Such a system does indeed give the taxpayer a strong incentive to co-operate.

The present system has its defenders, however; but that as late as 1972 it had apparently not been 'operated fully by computers' is itself a commentary on the administration. Some of those concerned with making the week-by-week adjustments have complained that it would be difficult to make end-year adjustments 'unless with computers'. Comment is superfluous.

OTHER FORMS OF INCOME SUPPLEMENTATION

The 1972 Tax Credit scheme

Proposals for a Tax Credit System was published as an official 'Green Paper' in 1972. But the claim has not been made, either for the Government 'Green Paper' proposals mentioned above, or for other Tax Credit proposals, that they would abolish

---

[1] 'Green Paper', *Proposals for a Tax Credit System*, HMSO, 1972.

poverty, or remove the need for the Supplementary Benefits Commission.

It was proposed in the Green Paper to issue

'to people who regularly work for an employer, to office-holders, to retirement pensioners and people in receipt of other National Insurance benefits, and to certain people who have retired from employment with an occupational pension',

credit cards which could be used in part-payment of income tax liabilities, or, where income tax liability was below the value of the credit cards, receivable in cash. The rates of credit then under discussion—the text making it clear that these must be regarded solely as 'illustrative'—were £4 per week for a single adult, £6 for a married couple, and £2 for a child. The gross value of payments at these rates would have been about £8 billion annually; but it was estimated that most of them would be paid in tax, leaving a net burden on the Revenue of £1.3 billion annually.

To convert from 1972 to present-day prices, the weekly value of the cards would have to be approximately doubled. An estimate of how much would now be recoverable in tax is not available.

This scheme would have the merit of simplifying administration, particularly by getting rid of the weekly adjustments of tax rates, laborious both for civil servants and for employers. It would also have the incidental effect of making National Insurance benefits taxable—'as was the original position under the National Insurance Scheme'.

The compilers of the Green Paper did not claim that their scheme would serve to displace any of the wide variety of means-tested and other social welfare schemes, except Family Income Supplement. The Green Paper pointed out (p. 5) that about 10 per cent of the adult population and their dependants would be outside the scheme. These would be principally the self-employed, some of whom are in need of help, as well as those earning very low or irregular wages, and other families clearly in poverty.

The Green Paper proposals were subjected to a thorough examination by a Parliamentary Select Committee in 1973. It appeared that a substantial part of the benefit from the net expenditure of £1.3 billion (at 1972 prices) would accrue to comparatively high-income taxpayers. This appears to have

[57]

been an inevitable consequence of the effort of those who framed the scheme to provide that no taxpayer should be any worse off than he had been before.

Giving evidence[1] before the Select Committee on Tax Credit, the Tax Credit Study Group estimated the distribution of the £1,300 million of net benefits as follows:

Income Range £/year	£ million
0–1,000	150
1,000–2,000	750
2,000–5,000	380
Over 5,000	45
	1,325

The income group below £1,000, they also pointed out, would include many single people, people working for only part of the year, and pensioners and other low-income families whose gains from Tax Credits would be partially or wholly offset by loss of FIS or supplementary benefit.

The Bow Group Tax Credit scheme

Much stronger proposals for tax credits have been made by the Bow Group.[2] Unlike the Green Paper, these proposals are designed to cover the entire population. As pointed out above, the amounts mentioned in the 1972 Green Paper would have to be approximately doubled to convert to present-day prices. They would have to be approximately doubled again to match the Bow Group proposals.

In the Bow Group proposals tax was to be levied at the rate of 40 per cent on all incomes, against which tax credits were to be allowed of £14 per week for a single adult, £21 for a married couple, widow or widower, and £7 for a child under 16. For single persons and married couples over the age of 65, the credits would be raised to £20 and £32 respectively. Table VII shows the amounts receivable under the different proposals at various levels of family income.

[1] 17 May 1973, p. 418.
[2] Andrew Dalton and others, *A Chancellor's Primer*, Bow Group, February 1976, p. 17.

TABLE VII

COMPARISON OF BOW GROUP (BG) AND REVERSE TAX (RT) PROPOSALS

(Reverse Tax including proposed annuity to aged)

Reverse Tax or net Tax Credit payable £ per household per week	Income from other sources £ per head per week							
	0		5		10		15	
	BG	RT	BG	RT	BG	RT	BG	RT
Single person below 65	14	13.7	12	10.2	10	6.7	8	3.2
Single person above 65	20	21.2	18	17.7	16	14.2	14	10.7
Married couple below 65	21	21.8	17	14.9	13	7.8	9	0.9
Married couple above 65	32	36.8	28	29.9	24	22.8	20	15.9
Married couple with 2 dependent children	35	32.9	27	18.9	19	4.8	11	0

The cost of the Bow Group proposals can be approximately estimated on the assumptions made above. Pre-tax personal incomes at the beginning of 1977, excluding employers' social security contributions, life insurance accruals, and all kinds of government pensions and benefits may be expected to be at the rate of £95 billion annually, giving a gross tax revenue of £38 billion. (With a few exceptions, the Bow Group proposals would give payments which would surpass all present benefits, and make them redundant.)

The value of the Bow Group tax credits is estimated for the projected 1977 UK population, with some extrapolations of the marital status tables.[1]

TABLE VIII

VALUE OF BOW GROUP TAX CREDITS, 1977

	Numbers in millions		Proposed weekly tax credits	
	Couples	Persons	Per couple or person £	Aggregate £ million
Married couples, husband over 65	2.3		32	74
All others over 65		3.4	20	68
Married couples, husband under 65	12.2		21	256
Widowed and divorced under 65		2.0	21	42
Other adults under 65		8.2	14	115
Children under 16		13.5	7	95
		56.1		650

The cost of the tax credits would be £650 million weekly or £34 billion annually, thus leaving a net return of only £4 billion. But the Bow Group proposals are expected to eliminate the need for practically all present social security payments. It is clear, nevertheless, that, even after large reductions in other

[1] *Annual Abstract of Statistics*, 1975, Tables 12–15.

government expenditures, indirect taxation would have to be much increased.

The Bow Group proposals would in some cases (i.e. single people over 65) still call for payments of public money to people with incomes up to £50 per week, or to married couples over 65 with combined incomes of £80 per week. The proposed tax rate of 40 per cent on all incomes is about the same as that now paid (if National Insurance contributions are included) by most earners: but this is generally admitted to be too high, and destructive of incentive. A rate of 30 per cent, however, would leave no net return at all. Against this disadvantage we may set the advantage of the lower 'cut-out' rate—40 instead of 70 per cent—for those receiving benefits.

A more fundamental criticism of the Bow Group proposals is that they impose no work test, and that the allowances are so high that many people would seek to live on them permanently—fervently agitating meanwhile for their increase.

REVERSE TAX AND GOVERNMENT REVENUE/EXPENDITURE

Finally, we relate the proposed expenditure on Reverse Tax and annuities, savings on social security expenditure, and new tax scales to the whole pattern of other public expenditure and revenue. Official forecasts of revenue and expenditure are available, but it is not clear on what assumptions about average earnings they are based. To accord with our assumption of earnings 25 per cent above the 1975 level, projections are made after examining revenue and expenditure figures for past years, restated in 1977 terms by using each year's average earnings figure. Projections are made of all central and local government revenues (duplication through grants to local governments being eliminated) other than personal income tax, and current (not capital) expenditure on objects other than social security (Table IX).

The interest and repayment of annuity bonds for old people, at the rate of £390 per head per year, would cost £3.1 billion per year, of which about a quarter would represent bonds paid for by the recipients. A net expense may arise during the transition period from those choosing Alternative (i) described above, i.e. continuing to pay present taxes and receive present benefits; its amount cannot be estimated.

As against the £17 billion required, the various possible tax

[60]

TABLE IX

CENTRAL GOVERNMENT AND LOCAL AUTHORITY (NOT PUBLIC CORPORATIONS) CURRENT ACCOUNTS: RESOURCES AND EXPENDITURES, 1970–76 AND PROJECTION OF 1977 PERSONAL INCOME TAX REQUIREMENT

	Actual: £ billion								Converted to estimated 1977 wage-rates: £ billion							
	1970	1971	1972	1973	1974	1975	1976[a]	1977	1970	1971	1972	1973	1974	1975	1976[a]	1977 Projected
Resources of Central Government:																
Corporation Tax	1.63	1.51	1.42	1.85	2.84	2.26	(2.2)		4.44	3.66	3.12	3.61	4.61	2.82	2.52	2.5
Expenditure Taxes	5.76	6.06	4.46	7.33	8.36	10.14	11.16		15.70	14.48	14.16	14.32	13.56	12.67	12.78	12.8
Employers' National Insurance Contributions	1.24	1.32	1.57	1.92	2.65	3.70	4.1[b]		3.38	3.20	3.45	3.75	4.30	4.62	4.60	5.6
All other[c]	2.39	2.39	2.31	2.15	2.46	3.06	3.96		6.78	5.79	5.07	4.20	3.99	3.82	4.54	4.5
Local Authority Revenue[d]	3.05	3.41	3.79	4.37	5.12	6.48	7.30		8.31	8.27	8.33	8.53	8.31	8.09	8.36	8.3
																33.7
Expenditures of Central Government:																
Defence	2.42	2.71	3.02	3.34	4.04	5.06	5.80		6.59	6.57	6.63	6.52	6.55	6.31	6.65	6.7
National Health	1.73	1.95	2.24	2.50	3.53	4.86	5.49		4.71	4.72	4.91	4.87	5.73	6.07	6.29	6.5
Debt Interest	1.30	1.38	1.58	1.76	2.11	2.64	3.22		3.54	3.35	3.47	3.43	3.42	3.29	3.69	4.0
Transfers to persons[e]	0.58	0.66	0.93	0.94	1.13	1.48	1.9[b]		1.58	1.60	2.04	1.83	1.84	1.85	2.18	2.2
All other[e,f]	2.22	2.50	2.92	3.55	5.38	7.02	7.36		6.05	6.06	6.40	6.93	8.73	8.77	8.44	8.5
Local Authorities' Current Expenditure	5.03	5.58	6.36	7.75	9.39	13.04	14.44		13.68	13.52	13.95	15.13	15.22	16.27	16.55	17.0
																44.9
Average Earnings (£)[g]	1,202	1,350	1,492	1,676	2,015	2,620	2,940	3,275								

Balance of above to be met   11.2
Cost of Reverse Tax   3.3
Interest and repayment on indexed annuity bonds   2.5

Balance to be met by personal income tax   17.0

[a] First half-year seasonally adjusted figures expressed as annual rate.
[b] Approximate estimate.
[c] Not personal income tax or employees' National Insurance contributions.
[d] Not grants from Central Government.
[e] Other than personal transfers proposed to be replaced by Reverse Tax.
[f] Excluding grants to Local Authorities.
[g] National Accounts wage and salary payments divided by numbers employed: 1976 calculated from Department of Employment index; 1977 at 25 per cent above 1975 to agree with calculations of cost of Reverse Tax, etc.

scales considered above (Table III) show a range of yields from £16.2 to £21.4 billion. Other reductions in government expenditure, which may well be expected, would make possible further reductions in personal income tax, or in other taxes.

What appears to have the strongest of all cases for tax reduction is a further allowance of 'inflation accounting' on business stocks and depreciation.

APPENDIX TO SECTION V

CALCULATIONS OF REVERSE TAX COSTS AND INCOME TAX YIELDS

National Income and Expenditure 1965–75 shows (Table 4.8) the distribution of personal incomes, but only for 'tax units', and for the year 1973–74. If we need detailed information on the distribution of incomes in relation to family size and structure the only good source is to be found (as was seen when the Treasury had to present evidence on this matter to the Parliamentary Select Committee on Tax Rebates in 1973) in the *Family Expenditure Survey* published annually by the Department of Employment. The latest issue refers to the calendar year 1975.

The *Family Expenditure Survey* is based on a sample, which appears reasonably representative when tested for age composition, and also for the proportion of self-employed heads of households.

The income in various categories recorded in the *Family Expenditure Survey* can be checked against the corresponding entries in *National Income and Expenditure*. These latter contain (discreetly veiled) estimates of the extent of tax evasion. It is reasonable to suppose that a household which has under-declared its income for taxation would also understate it for the Survey.

Table X shows very wide discrepancies for self-employment, less so for investment income, and only slight for wage and salary income.

The cause of the discrepancy in Social Security income becomes apparent when we study the detailed components for 1974, and also the instructions for recording income in the *Family Expenditure Survey*. Choosing an (unavoidably) arbitrary limit of 13 weeks, the Department of Employment instructed compilers to ignore absence from work through sickness or unemployment for durations below

[62]

TABLE X

PERSONAL INCOMES, 1974 AND 1975
Differences in Estimates Reflecting Tax Evasion
(£ per head of population)[a]

	1974 National Accounts (Table 4.1)	1974 Family Expenditure Survey (Table 35)	Ratio	1975 National Accounts (Table 4.1)	1975 Family Expenditure Survey (Table 35)	Ratio
Wages and Salaries[b]	839.9	778.2	1.08	1,082.0	1,011.2	1.07
Self-employment	191.0	80.7	1.74	155.4	74.8	2.08
Investment[c]	95.6	77.5	1.23	107.9	92.9	1.16
Other		37.4			43.4	
Social Security	140.6	100.4	1.40	182.3	129.8	1.40
TOTAL	1,216.1	1,074.4	1.13	1,527.6	1,351.1	1.13
Social Security details[d]						
Retirement pensions	62.3	59.8	1.09	80.0		
Widows' pensions	5.4	5.6	0.97	6.9		
Unemployment benefit	4.1	2.8	1.46	7.1		
Sickness and injury benefit	12.8	5.3	2.41	15.9		
Maternity benefit	0.8	0.7	1.14	0.9		
Death grant	0.3	—	—	0.3		
Family Allowances	6.9	7.0	0.92	8.9		
Supplementary benefits	15.6	14.1	1.11	19.7		
Disablement benefits	2.0	—	—	2.4		

a 56 million in both years.
b Including HM Forces. Not including employers' national insurance contributions.
c Excluding receipts by life insurance and superannuation funds. Including sub-letting and imputed income from owner-occupancy.
d *National Accounts*, Tables 7.1 and 7.4. Family Expenditure Survey details for 1974 from *Economic Trends*, February 1976, p. 93. Figures given per household and converted to per person (6,695 households and 18,974 persons). Corresponding figures for 1975 not yet available. Not including disablement benefits and war pensions which are combined with private pensions in other incomes.

this limit, i.e. to record the person's normal earnings. Sickness and unemployment benefits received, except in absences from work for more than 13 weeks, were correspondingly omitted from the record. It is in these categories that the largest discrepancies between *National Income and Expenditure* and *Family Expenditure Survey* are to be found.

Estimate of tax evasion

If incomes received had been recorded, social security benefits would have been, in 1974, some £9 per head higher than shown. Earned incomes would have been lower by something in the neighbourhood of £20 per head—depending upon our estimate of the average ratio between normal earnings and unemployment or sickness benefit. The ratio between the aggregates, shown in the last column, should therefore be about 1.14 instead of 1.13.

It is not, however, intended to apply this rough estimate of the extent of tax evasion in making the calculations of the cost of a Reverse Tax scheme, or of yields from a revised system of income tax. If tax evasion prevails now, it is also likely to prevail for some time into the future, both for tax assessment and in claims for Reverse Tax.

In the calculations which follow, all incomes are taken at 25 per cent above 1975 levels (see text above). It was assumed also that there had been no significant changes since 1975 in income distribution, or in total population.

The income data as recorded are accepted, at 'normal' rates of earning for people out of work because of sickness or unemployment of less than 13 weeks' duration. In other words, in most of such cases, if the family had recourse to Reverse Tax at all, it would only be temporarily, to be repaid within a few months. Families with incomes disrupted by sickness or unemployment for longer periods would, however, be expected to be claimants for Reverse Tax. The numbers who happen to be included during the weeks in which the Survey is taken are regarded (as with other family characteristics) as an adequate sample. Likewise there is no need to adjust the records of Social Security receipts in the *Family Expenditure Survey* (inadequate for the reasons given). The amounts shown are deducted from total income, to estimate incomes exclusive of present Social Security receipts. These are to be the basis for estimating the cost of Reverse Tax, and the yields from revised income tax.

A detailed cross-tabulation is made for 16 ranges of family income (from all sources), and for 19 family types. The detailed cross-classification by incomes and family types is given in *Family Expenditure Survey*, Table 45, and the numbers of persons can be deduced from information in Table 44. The Social Security element in these incomes is, however, only given elsewhere, in Tables 6–15, in most cases for broader income-groups, so that detailed interpolation is necessary. These latter tables make an important further distinction, not shown in Table 45, for single persons and for one-man/one-woman households between those in which the head of the household is above or below age 65.

For a limited number of households (3 per cent of the total), containing four adults or more, shown at the foot of Table 45, no direct information on the Social Service component of their incomes is available. It has therefore to be estimated by difference between the Social Security receipt for all other families so far analysed, and the estimated total (£50,400 weekly for a total of 7,203 households in the sample).

[64]

VI. SUMMARY

1. Social security cost £9.6 billion in 1975, a 30 per cent increase over the previous year, with every prospect of similar increases in the future. For many men the levels of social security payments now constitute a discouragement to employment. It is indeed surprising that 'voluntary' unemployment is not more prevalent than it is.

2. Only drastic surgery can deal with this situation. It is proposed
   —that unemployment benefit, sickness benefit, supplementary benefit, retirement pension and some other services be progressively abolished, and replaced by Reverse Tax;
   —that there should be large reductions of personal income tax in all income groups, particularly for families with children, with a maximum marginal rate of 50 per cent; and
   —that employees' National Insurance contribution be abolished.

3. Under the Reverse Tax proposed here, 'basic' incomes would be fixed (at 1977 income levels) of £1,015 for a single person, £1,625 for a married couple without children, with an extra £406 for each dependent child. At or below these levels no income tax would be imposed, and any family receiving less would be entitled to a payment of 7/10ths of the amount by which their income fell below 'basic' income. If they were paid the full amount of the deficiency they would lose the incentive to earn. Under these proposals they would, in effect, keep 3/10ths of additional earnings. It would, of course, be desirable to allow them a larger fraction, but this would make the scheme inordinately costly; and moreover it would cover a large proportion of the entire wage-earning population.

4. Family incomes would have to be aggregated, both for Reverse Tax and for income tax purposes. The amount due would be finally calculated at the end of the tax year, when the family income was precisely known. A family in need could, however, apply for immediate assistance during the year, at rates not exceeding (at 1977 income levels) £28 per week for a single person or married couple

[65]

without children, £32.80 for a married couple with two dependent children, £43.80 for a married couple with four dependent children, etc. If the amounts so received during temporary unemployment or illness were found at the end of the year to have exceeded the amount to which the family was entitled, the surplus would be repayable, in most cases simply by withholding the refund of past weekly contributions normally due. If a family with income a long way above 'basic' applied for temporary assistance, the amount would be repayable at a penalty rate.

5. Older people would be able to make claims if they were below 'basic' income levels. In addition, they would be provided with government bonds, indexed against price increases, to provide additional income of £7.50 weekly. Any with substantial property would be expected to purchase these bonds themselves; those owning lesser amounts of property would share the cost. Persons approaching retirement age would be given a limited right to purchase these indexed bonds, which would not be immediately available to the general public.

6. The introduction of such a scheme at one blow would be administratively and politically out of the question. It is therefore proposed, in effect, to create a new class of taxpayers, to which no-one would be transferred except at his own request, though new taxpayers (young people, immigrants, etc.) would be placed in it. Taxpayers in this class would pay tax at much lower rates, and would be exempted from employees' National Insurance contributions, but would have to renounce all claims to unemployment benefits, sickness benefit, supplementary benefits, etc., on present scales. If they got into difficulties, they would have a claim (at lower rates) to the proposed Reverse Tax scales. Older people would be able to purchase the indexed bonds for annuities. People continuing to claim current social security benefits would have to produce evidence that they were still paying tax at the old rate. Transfer to the new class of taxpayer, once requested, could not be reversed.

7. People claiming Reverse Tax for prolonged periods on grounds of illness would be required to show medical

certificates, and on the grounds of unemployment, sub-jected to work tests. The Reverse Tax system is not designed to meet the needs of the disabled or of permanent invalids.

8. The cost of making such Reverse Tax payments at 1977 income levels, if all present social security payments were removed, would be £3.3 billion per year plus approx-imately £2.5 billion per year for annuities (interest and repayment on indexed bonds) to the aged. If all other forms of government expenditure and revenue continue on their present trends, and if government and local authority current accounts are to be balanced (borrowing to continue for capital works only), with the costs specified above for Reverse Tax and indexed bonds, employees' national insurance contributions having been abolished, a yield of £17 billion from personal income tax in 1977 would be required. Various tax scales on the principles given above, i.e. no tax at or below 'basic' incomes, and maximum marginal rate 50 per cent, are shown, with yields in the £16–£21 billion range.

9. Reverse Tax is very different from 'Tax Credits'. Reverse Tax would only be payable to people with low incomes. 'Tax Credits', on the other hand, would be payable to everyone (or nearly everyone), with the intention that those on higher incomes should use them to offset part of their tax liabilities, which would then be imposed at high marginal rates. The official 'Green Paper' tax credit proposals of 1972 were estimated (at that time) to cost £1.3 billion, much of which would have accrued to higher-income taxpayers, while leaving nearly 10 per cent of the population unprovided for. The much more extensive tax credit scheme recently proposed by the Bow Group has the 'credits' so high that even a 40 per cent tax on all incomes would leave hardly any net revenue and immense increases in indirect taxation would become necessary.

10. The ultimate object is for people to pay charges for some or all of what they receive in education, health, pension rights, etc.

QUESTIONS FOR DISCUSSION

1. What is meant by 'Reverse Tax' and why is it thought to have advantages over the current tax and social security systems?

2. What are the chief defects of the current system?

3. Should help be given to the poor by cash or *via* subsidies for individual services such as housing rents?

4. What is the difference between Tax Credits and Reverse Tax?

5. Why would Reverse Tax have to be based upon the family rather than upon the individual?

6. What is the 'cut-out' rate and why is its level so important to the scheme?

7. How would the Reverse Tax scheme deal with the old?

8. What precautions would be necessary to ensure that the Reverse Tax scheme is not abused?

9. How would the Reverse Tax scheme deal with the 'poverty-trap'?

10. What transition problems do you see in moving from the current system to Reverse Tax?

FURTHER READING

Aaron, H. J., *Why is Welfare so Hard to Reform?*, The Brookings Institution, Washington, DC, 1973.

Christopher, Anthony, Polanyi, George, Seldon, Arthur, and Shenfield, Barbara, *Policy for Poverty*, Research Monograph 20, Institute of Economic Affairs, 1970.

Friedman, Milton, *Capitalism and Freedom*, University of Chicago Press, Chicago, 1962.

Harris, Ralph and Seldon, Arthur, *Choice in Welfare 1970*, Institute of Economic Affairs, 1971.

Hayhoe, B., *Must the Children Suffer?*, Conservative Political Centre, London, 1968.

Howell, Ralph, *Why Work?*, Conservative Political Centre, London, 1976.

Proposals for a Tax Credit System, Cmnd. 5116, HMSO, London, 1972.

Rhys-Williams, B., *The New Social Contract*, Conservative Political Centre, London, 1967.

Seldon, Arthur, and Gray, Hamish, *Universal or Selective Social Benefits?*, Research Monograph 8, Institute of Economic Affairs, 1967.

Seldon, Arthur, *Taxation and Welfare*, Research Monograph 14, Institute of Economic Affairs, 1967.

Supplementary Benefits Commission, *Annual Report 1975*, Cmnd. 6615, HMSO, London, 1976.

Atkinson, A. B., *The Tax Credit Scheme and the Redistribution of Income*, Institute for Fiscal Studies (Publication No. 9), London, 1973.

Institute for Fiscal Studies, *Conference on Proposals for a Tax-Credit System*, IFS Publication No. 5, 1973.

Polanyi, G. and P., 'Tax Credits: A Reverse Income Tax', *National Westminster Bank Quarterly Review*, February 1973.

Some IEA Papers on TAXATION

Hobart Paper 26
Taxmanship
COLIN CLARK
1964 2nd Edition 1970 40p
'Perhaps the most debated question of the day is whether rising wages or rising prices are mainly responsible for inflation.'
Southern Evening Echo

Readings 4
Taxation: A Radical Approach
VITO TANZI, BARRY BRACEWELL-MILNES and D. R. MYDDELTON
1970 90p
'The three essays together illustrate clearly that sharply differential rates, both of direct and indirect taxation, increase the awareness and consequently the "burden" of taxation, and lose revenue. They make a strong case for a shift towards flatter rates of taxation.'
Accountancy

Hobart Paper 72
Over-taxation by Inflation
A study of the effects of inflation on taxation and government expenditure, and of its correction by indexing
DAVID R. MORGAN
1977 £1.50
'An extremely clear exposition of what has happened [has been] published by the Institute of Economic Affairs. It is a pamphlet called *Over-taxation by Inflation*, by Dr. David Morgan . . . No-one who has read Dr. Morgan's pamphlet can fail to be convinced by the argument.'
John Pardoe, *Hansard*, 3 March, 1977

Readings 16
The State of Taxation
A. R. PREST, COLIN CLARK, WALTER ELKAN, CHARLES K. ROWLEY, BARRY BRACEWELL-MILNES, IVOR F. PEARCE
with an Address by LORD HOUGHTON
1977 £2.00

Hobart Paper 73
Poverty before Politics
A study in a Reverse Income Tax
COLIN CLARK
1977 £1.50

IEA OCCASIONAL PAPERS in print